S E X U A L
HARASSMENT
IN SCHOOLS

A Guide for Teachers

SEXUAL HARASSMENT IN SCHOOLS

A Guide for Teachers

CARRIE HERBERT

David Fulton Publishers

London

David Fulton Publishers Ltd
2 Barbon Close, London WC1N 3JX

First published in Great Britain by
David Fulton Publishers 1992

Note: The right of the author to be identified as the author of this work has been asserted by her in accordance with the Copyright, Designs and Patents Act 1988.

Copyright © Carrie M. H. Herbert

British Library Cataloguing in Publication Data

   Herbert, Carrie M. H.
      Sexual harassment in schools : a guide for teachers.
      I Title
      362.7044

      ISBN 1-85346-192-X

Cover illustration by Catherine McConville ©
courtesy of Spellbound Card Co, 23 - 25 Moss Street, Dublin 2, Ireland (01-712149)

Typeset by the Author
Designed by Almac Ltd., London
Printed in Great Britain by Bell and Bain Ltd., Glasgow

Contents

Acknowledgements

I should like to thank all the people who have helped me develop the ideas for this book. In particular I pay tribute to the South Australian Department of Education, Adelaide, where many of these ideas began their life. My appreciation goes to the staff of Westbourne High School, Ipswich, Suffolk and the teachers on the Sexual Harassment Course at the Cambridge Institute of Education, June 1991, whose ideas, questions and challenges gave me food for thought and change. I thank Charlotte Moore, Samidha Williamson, Robert Evans, Caroline Paing, Margot Hurst and Jessica Feinstein for the useful contributions they made in terms of ideas, resources, information and editing. I wish to thank Rebecca and Laura for their help in providing data from primary schools. Finally, I am indebted to Ruth Loshak who gave unlimited personal and practical support as well as critical and pertinent comments when necessary throughout the writing of this book.

© Posy Simmonds (The Guardian)
Permission granted by Peters Frazer and Dunlop Ltd

Introduction

This book has been written especially with teachers, parents and students in mind to give access to information and ideas collected over the years which I have found useful when working with people on the issue of sexual harassment. It is a book which looks at the problem of sexual harassment from a broad perspective, placing it within the context of a Western industrialised society, describing how such behaviour is produced, reproduced and maintained throughout all classes, age groups and locations. Its most important function is to look at ways in which sexual harassment can be challenged within the school system. It is not a recipe book, however, with step-by-step instructions, nor does it contain 'tricks of the week', nor is it designed to be followed through from the beginning to the end. For this reason, some of the main arguments are repeated in different places, hopefully without boring the reader.

One problem is that as sexual harassment is not mentioned in the National Curriculum it might be thought that there is no time to deal with it. It is true that sexual harassment is not directly addressed, but the documents are very clear in their commitment to providing equal opportunities for all students and in their recommendation that students be prepared for life in a democratic society (NCC, 1990). If these aims are to be achieved the eradication of all forms of harassment, including sexual harassment, from all areas of the school will be necessary.

The National Curriculum makes it clear that there is much scope for education about equal opportunities in Education for Citizenship (NCC, 1990). Whether issues of equal opportunities are dealt with within other subjects such as English, History, Social Studies or Religious Education, or whether they are taught within the Personal and Social Education programme will be an individual school decision. However, it is recommended that once a decision has been made to address issues of sexual harassment, as wide and comprehensive a programme as possible be employed. Thus a three pronged initiative is proposed. A policy will need to be developed which will take as one of its main objectives the consciousness-raising of staff, students, parents and governors. Simultaneously it will be necessary to deal with incidents of sexual harassment when they arise in classroom, corridor or street. This can be a valuable method of learning about sexual harassment for all involved. Thirdly, there will need to be a curriculum initiative, in which issues of equal opportunities are located in a far broader framework than just sexual harassment, so that students can see how and why such behaviour has, until recently, been accepted, seen as normal and remained unchallenged. Topics such as the role of women in society, in fairy stories, in literature, in advertising, in the Bible, in mathematics, or in history could be looked at in many different subject areas, at all ages.

There is nothing prescriptive about this book, because learning must be in the hands of the learners, whether that is you learning to teach about sexual harassment, or the students learning about the issues. As a teacher you know how you prefer to work and whether you like to encourage the learners to use role play, discussions, written work, debates, drama or other processes when coming to understanding. Learning which comes about because one is personally committed and engaged in the issues is my preferred model. I know this is how I learn best, and think this is true of other learners too. Learning about sexual harassment will not be effective if the students are told what to think about the topic, if restrictions and procedures are forced upon them, or if they are not committed or interested. Attitudes and values associated with the perpetuation of sexual harassment cannot be changed overnight.

The book is divided into two main sections. The first three chapters deal with sexual harassment as a phenomenon and describe how the combination of individual power and institutional power provides the structure for this behaviour to be perpetuated. There are also discussions on the ways in which the traditions and mores of our society enable sexual harassment to be reproduced and maintained in each successive generation, as children are brought up to conform to stereotyping and to accept this particular unwanted attention as normal. It is my contention that as sexual harassment is learned behaviour it can be unlearned.

In Chapters 4, 5 and 6, the second section, the same themes of individual and institutional power are continued. However, in these three chapters I look at ways of addressing sexual harassment at both the institutional level and at a personal level. Sexual harassment can be addressed within institutions by writing and implementing a policy and by introducing aspects of this topic into all curriculum areas. The third chapter in this section discusses ways of dealing with sexual harassment at an individual level.

There are also two appendices. The first offers further information about sexual harassment in the form of myths and vignettes. These may be useful as discussion starters which could, with negotiation, lead on to a much longer programme of study. The second appendix contains extracts from classical literature, historical information, and some modern poetry which can be used as discussion points for all those engaged in learning about the issues of sexual harassment. Last, there is included a list of non-sexist books suitable for students at all levels.

Whilst writing this book I have been showered with anecdotes of sexual harassment from friends, colleagues and even strangers whom I have met and talked with about my work. I have included some of these, to illustrate the frequency and varied nature of sexual harassment, as well as to indicate the wide range of different recipients to whom it occurs. Because sexual harassment comes in so many guises and can be particularly subtle, it is not always easy at first to recognise a particular behaviour as such. So I begin the book with an example of elusive sexual harassment given to me only recently. A woman teacher was taking a 5 year old boy to the sick room because he was not feeling well. He was holding her hand. As they passed the headteacher's office the head spoke to the little boy, whilst ignoring the teacher. He said, 'You had better enjoy holding that lady's hand, Johnny, because when you are as old as me you won't be allowed to.' I am sure that for some people this will be regarded as an innocuous remark, but I label it sexual harassment. Why I call this behaviour sexual harassment and the implications it has for women and girls, as well as men and boys, will, I hope, become clear in the following chapters as the book unfolds.

Individual and Institutional Power

CHAPTER 1

Definitions

Introduction

This chapter discusses sexual harassment as a phenomenon within our society and shows how it is the combination of institutional and individual power which makes it effective as a controlling strategy. Throughout parts of the text I have added questions, pieces of information and other details and put them in boxes. This is done to draw attention to aspects of the argument or issues which could be discussed or dealt with so that learners become aware of the social forces which maintain and perpetuate sexual harassment, as well as tapping into knowledge and experiences of their own. They have not been designed to be used as one-off exercises, but as part of an educational programme to challenge and change attitudes and values. It is important to realise too, that if they are used as individual exercises, without careful consideration of the needs and interests of the group, they are likely to achieve nothing more than aggressive behaviour by the group members and an even greater adherence to stereotyped beliefs about the role of women and men in our society.

Sexual harassment: not a new phenomenon

Sexual harassment is not a new phenomenon, for the term encompasses behaviour which has been practised for centuries. Until recently this way of treating women was considered by many people, both men and women, to be acceptable. In 1968 an American lecturer, Lyn Farley, discussing employment issues with a group of women, recognised that unwanted attention was a constant problem at work. She noted that it was detrimental and oppressive, and labelled it 'sexual harassment'. In the book she wrote in 1978, Lyn Farley describes how the women on her course talked about their bosses and other male colleagues patting and touching them, making sexual innuendoes and propositions and in some cases sexually assaulting them. Because they were all employees, because of their invidious position *vis-à-vis* their bosses, they felt intimidated and embarrassed and compromised. They also felt unable to do anything about it, for fear of reprisals, making the problem worse, being sacked without a reference, and being accused of provocation. Because of the sexual harassment many decided to leave their jobs and look for another one.

Discussion
Discuss and share your own experiences of unwanted sexual attention, given or received. Do this in single sex groups. What happened?
Discuss any differing perspectives of males and females to the discussion.
Aim: to see how frequent cases of sexual harassment have been within the group, what people felt about the unwanted attention and to share strategies for stopping the behaviour.

Sexual harassment: what is it?

Sexual harassment is unsolicited and unreciprocated behaviour (sometimes of a sexual nature or with sexual overtones) towards people in less powerful positions or circumstances. Because of the learned mores and traditions in our society, sexual harassment is often confused with what is considered natural behaviour and as such is regarded as normal and unremarkable by many people. It may include an explicit or implicit threat of discriminatory action which can be of a non-sexual nature, such as failing a course, or might involve displeasure for non-compliance.

Whilst some individual incidents can be extremely serious, much sexual harassment causes low-level irritation and embarrassment. The hand on the shoulder, or the lecherous leer, is by itself of no particularly importance, and to complain of an isolated incident or attitude such as this is often seen by many men, and women too, to be excessively petty. However, there are two points to be made. First, whilst that action in itself may seem to be harmless, behind the leer or the unwanted pat is a far more subtle and insidious threat of further and more serious sexual harassment. Second, this type of belittling is not isolated, but happens, particularly to girls in schools, many times during the school day. Continuous or frequent sexual harassment hits at the heart of girls' and women's self-image, casting them always in the role of sexual object and denying them the right to personhood.

Sexual harassment is an expression of power and is generally not motivated by sexual desire. An harasser may claim that a girl's or woman's behaviour is enticing, her clothes are provocative, or that he thought she was flirting with him, in order to justify his aggressive actions. These claims puts the onus of responsibility for the harassment on to the woman or girl, implying that she liked it. If it were the case that the woman wanted sexual attention and had sought it by behaving in a particular way or wearing particular clothes, then this would not be sexual harassment. Sexual harassment is unwanted, unwelcome and unsolicited.

Discussion
In single-sex groups discuss the difference between sexual harassment and flirting.
<u>Aim</u>: to see how close the behaviour called sexual harassment and wanted sexual attention can be when taken out of context.

Women and girls may well believe that certain clothes or behaviours are provocative or enticing - in fact they are taught to dress 'attractively' and act 'pleasantly'. They might therefore think that treatment of an unwanted kind is caused by their behaviour or the clothes they wear. But as sexual harassment is usually practised with little regard for the appearance or behaviour of the recipient, this is an unwarranted assumption.

Whilst sexual harassment is largely seen as a problem within the workplace, it can and does occur in many more places than this. Sexual harassment is the combination of two types of power: individual and institutional power working in conjunction. Its powerful effect results from an individual's behaviour being condoned and sanctioned by society's traditions, customs and attitudes. In our society, as with many others, men as a group hold more power and authority than women. One of the terms used to describe the overarching domination of women by men is 'patriarchy'. 'Patriarchy' describes a complex and multi-level process of power distribution located both in interpersonal relationships and within the institutional structure. If men and women were truly equal in all aspects of life, sexual harassment could not exist. In order to fully appreciate why sexual harassment is a problem, it is necessary to understand how patriarchal power survives and is reproduced through individuals and institutions within our society.

Discussion
In single-sex groups discuss the section entitled:
Sexual harassment: what is it?
Aim: To encourage the students to critique and to discuss the different issues in this definition.

Individual power

The ability to use power at a personal level can be seen to be unequal for women and men, boys and girls. How is this to be explained?

Discussion
Read: *The Paperbag Princess* by Robert Munsch (1982).
Who has the power in this story?
How is it used?
Why is this story different from most other stories about princesses, princes and dragons?
Make up some other stories in this style.

Boys 'inherit' more individual power than girls when they are born. They may not choose to exercise this power but it is automatically invested in them. Whilst this phenomenon is not as overt or extreme as it used to be, many laws equalising aspects of the legal system have only just been changed and there are still remnants of men's inherited authority over women today in British traditions and customs. For example, at a Christian wedding celebration a bride is usually 'given away' to the bridegroom. Is it the assumption that because a daughter is 'owned' by her father she can be 'given' to another man, her husband? When she signs the marriage register a woman often, as a matter of course, takes her husband's last name. Until 1990, married women were not allowed to be taxed separately from their husbands, in effect ensuring the husband knew what his wife earned and could have some controlling influence. Until 1991, a wife could not claim that she had been raped by her husband. As the law stood, once married a man could use his wife in a sexual way without her consent. Women can only succeed to the British throne if there is no male heir. A similar condition applies to knighthoods, peerages and dukedoms. Women cannot be fully ordained as priests in the Church of England or Roman Catholic Church nor in the Muslim, Jewish or Hindu faiths.

Research and discussion
Find out the arguments for and against women being ordained as priests?
In small groups discuss your own feelings.
Aim: for students/adults to understand the way in which our culture maintains stereotyped views of what are appropriate roles for women and men.

The difference in the individual power which men and women hold can often be seen more clearly in other cultures. However, that is not to say that sexism or sexual discrimination exists to any less degree here, it's just that because we are so used to it, it is sometimes more difficult to recognise. In China, because parents have until recently only been allowed one child, some girl infants were killed at birth because a boy was traditionally considered of more use and value.

Newspaper cutting for discussion
'China's peasants are allowed to have more than one child if the first is a daughter under a policy intended in part to stop the killing of baby girls, Mr Peiyus, the Family Planning Minister said yesterday.
"Abandonment and drowning of baby girls has not completely disappeared in China", he said.
"In the countryside, peasants always want a boy. If they have got a daughter, but still have the chance to have another baby, this helps them stop abandoning baby girls"'.
The Times (7th September 1988, p.6).
Aim: to discuss why boy babies are more wanted than girl babies.

In India, similarly, it appears that boy babies are considered more valuable because of their earning capacity. Also, families traditionally have to find large dowries for their daughters when they marry. In 1988 it was reported that some Indian women were flying to London to have an amniocentesis. From this test they could ascertain whether the embryo was male or female and in some cases it was decided to abort the baby because it was not the 'right' sex.

Newspaper cutting for discussion
'Doctors are carrying out illegal tests to discover the sex of unborn babies and then offering abortions to mothers who are under cultural pressure to give birth to boys. Dr. R. Verma, Senior Lecturer in Gynaecology and Obstetrics at St George's Hospital, Tooting, London, has been approached by Asian women willing to pay large sums to discover their baby's sex and then have an abortion if it is not what they want'.
The Times (4th January 1988, p.3).
Aim: to discuss the perceived need for women to have boy babies and the difficult situation of whether women have the
right to an abortion depending on the sex of their baby.

In some Westernised countries such as Great Britain, Australia and Western Germany, there is a growing market for Philippino wives. These women can be bought through mail order catalogues. Individual men are able to 'purchase' wives.

The women who apply for such marriages are often well educated but find it impossible to gain good employment in their own country. The notion of romantic love and marriage to a wealthy white Western man is promoted as a desirable accomplishment for these women.

However, the reality of marriage to a man from a different religion and culture, who is a virtual stranger, who is usually many years older and has a previous marriage and grown up children, is very different to this dream. Philippino women often have little English (or German) language, are isolated from their friends, their family and their church, cannot get work visas and are therefore totally dependent on their new husband for love, money, friends, family, entertainment and education. Their personal power is negligible.

The reason that the interviewed men say they desire women of this kind, however, is that Philippino women are more 'feminine'. For 'feminine' I think it must be implicitly understood that these men are looking for women who are more submissive, nurturing, attentive, caring, and who have a more expressed interest in domestic work than many Western women today.

Newspaper cutting for discussion
Advertisements such as these appear in many British local papers.
'PHILIPPINE LADIES. We have many Philippine ladies aged between 18 to 45, looking for friendship and marriage. For free details send SAE to...'

The training and conditioning which boys and girls receive underlies the substantial difference between males and females in authority and power. Gender-role models are presented to children as desirable, and children willingly take them on. I say 'willingly' because children (as do adults) like to conform and to feel they belong to a particular group. The pressure to assent to one's assigned gender is extremely strong. By the time they are adults children know the values, attitudes and skills associated with their gender-role and will be maintaining the traditional and cultural inequality. Further, they will probably in later years, when they have their own children, perpetuate the *status quo*.

Discussion
Think of a time in your childhood when you were told you couldn't do something because of your gender. What did you do at the time?
Who else was involved? What did you feel at the time?
What do you feel now?
Share experiences and compare feelings with others in your group.
Aim: to compare incidents of gender-stereotyping in childhood in order to discuss the seriousness and implications of such events.

Once adult, men have their individual power boosted and their authority maintained over individual women in a variety of ways. On average men earn more money than women and are more likely to hold jobs with authority and status. In a work situation more women are managed by men, than men are managed by women, or women are managed by women. Managerial positions provide men with the opportunity to develop skills and experience in the world of commerce, politics and society giving them more personal authority and consequently more confidence.

Personal self-esteem and confidence are often dependent on status gained from a respected position in the workplace. Although 54% of women work and represent 40% of all workers, they occupy many of the lower-paid jobs, are part-time, have little union affiliation and are the least protected of workers.

Facts
99% of secretaries are women
85% of managing directors are men
4% of High Court judges are women
95% of surgeons are men
49% of teachers in secondary schools are women
85% of headteachers in secondary schools are men
82% of shop assistants are women
95% of bank managers are men
91% of office cleaners are women
87% of nurses are women
97% of hand machinists in the textile industry are women

Another area in which men have more individual power than women is in their personal relationships. Women usually, although not always, marry men who are older, better qualified, and economically more viable than themselves. These attributes give men privileges, which are often not questioned for they are thought to be normal and natural advantages. It is considered appropriate that a woman should marry a more experienced, financially secure, mature man who can protect her, offer guidance to her and take responsibility for her throughout her life. However, in return for marrying men such as these, women are usually expected to 'service' their husbands.

Research

Over a week, monitor the people who do the domestic work in your house. Find out who organises the work. Who does what? How long does it take each person?

Aim: to find out how domestic labour is divided in some homes in Britain.

Women, whether in paid employment or not, are often responsible for household management, caring for children, cleaning, shopping, cooking and organising the social life of the family. This unpaid work has to be done outside paid work hours, usually in the evenings and at weekends. Whilst some men do help in the house, the helping is usually as a favour and not as a self-instigated co-houseworker.

In conclusion, individually, men are seen to be entitled to be looked after, to deserve better and more important jobs, to earn more money than women, to be in more secure and authoritative positions, with stronger union representation and better working conditions. These benefits men gain, not because they are individually better than individual women but because of the way in which society is constructed. The privileged position gives them the power base necessary to use sexual harassment as a method of control.

Institutional power

Inequality is reflected not only in the personal and individual advantages men have, but also in the institutions which invest men with more power and authority. Men are socially, economically and educationally advantaged owing to the structure of the society in which we live. As Kate Millett (1977, p.25) says '... our society, like all other historical civilisations, is a patriarchy. The fact is evident at once if one recalls that the military, industry, technology, universities, science, political office, finance - in short, every avenue of power within the society, including the coercive force of the police, is entirely in male hands'.

Facts
Dates in selected countries where women were first entitled to vote:

New Zealand	1893	Finland	1906
Norway	1913	Poland	1918
Sweden	1919	Netherlands	1919
Germany	1919	U.S.A.	1920
U.K.	1928	Brazil	1932
Turkey	1934	France	1944
Belgium	1948	Greece	1952
Switzerland	1971	Liechtenstein	1984

Patriarchy as an institution is deeply entrenched and frames all political, social and economic activity, including class, caste, bureaucracy and all major religions, although its form and style varies in different historical contexts and locations. In Western democracies women hold very few political positions, the British Parliament for example, being represented by approximately 14% of women members, in a country where 51% of the population is female.

Facts
Dates in selected countries where women were first appointed to cabinet:

Poland	1918	Sweden	1947
New Zealand	1947	Finland	1926
Greece	1956	U.K.	1929
U.S.A.	1933	Norway	1945
France	1947	Turkey	1971
Netherlands	1956	West Germany	1961
Belgium	1965	Switzerland	1971
Brazil	1971	Liechtenstein	1984

The schooling system is an institution which discriminates between girls and boys. Teachers, usually unintentionally and unconsciously, encourage boys to be leaders, to make decisions and to succeed.

Research

Appoint two students as recorders.
Ask them to write down the names of all the people who speak during your lesson, approximately how long they speak and what type of talking it is: question asking, question answering, interruption, reprimand, etc.
Discuss your results.

Research by Dale Spender (1982) has shown that teachers ask more searching questions of boys, pick them to lead debates, are more likely to challenge their thinking and their attitudes and are likely to read to the whole class stories which have male protagonists for role models.

Research

Collect a copy of every novel from one year level. Make a note of:
the sex of the author, the sex of the main character and the sex of the secondary character.
What do you find? Discuss your results in a small group.

In a mixed school the administration is often male-dominated, reflecting the management structure of society. One of the results of the imbalance in education is that boys leave school with qualifications which will provide them with access to those jobs which our society endorses as important.

Activity

Ask the children to draw pictures of:
- a scientist
- a nurse
- a mechanic
- a teacher
- a dentist
- a receptionist
- a doctor
- a secretary

In small groups ask them to show their drawings to others and discuss their findings.
Aim: to encourage children to discuss the jobs which are available and to understand that both men and women can train for any career.

Statistics GCSE Examination Results in thousands: Source: *School Examination Survey*, D.E.S., 1988/89.		
Subject	Girls	Boys
English Language	277.5	274.8
Maths	263.8	268.5
Biology	135.1	81.9
French	148.5	106.3
Music/Drama	44.4	26.4
History	109.5	108.9
Chemistry	79.2	99.8
Physics	58.0	138.9
Computer Science	21.7	45.3

Our society gives primacy to the acquisition of material wealth, personal status, professional expertise and ambition. The professional jobs in law, medicine, business, economics and politics provide these. More boys than girls are likely to leave school with the requisite and appropriate qualifications, an intended career structure, confidence, professional and parental support and high personal expectations to pursue these goals successfully.

Statistics Advanced Level attempts and passes in thousands: Source: *School Examination Survey*, D.E.S., 1988/89.				
Subject	Girls' Attempts	Girls' Passes	Boys' Attempts	Boys' Passes
English	28.6	24.8	13.7	12.0
Maths	18.0	14.1	33.5	25.5
Physics	7.6	5.9	25.3	20.0

The values and attitudes embedded in the institutions (where the myths are that men will be the major wage earners and look after their wives, and that women will get married, have babies and stay at home), are mirrored in the more readily accessible entry males have into powerful positions in the workplace. Banks, universities, government offices, multi-national corporations, law and accountancy firms all recruit young men with the expectation that one of them will, in due course, take over the chair, the ministry, or the partnership.

Sexual harassment depends on institutional and individual power working together. Separately, these two power sources are not as effective or coercive, nor are they regarded as being so normal, unremarkable or idiosyncratic for a man, if they operate alone.

Can men be sexually harassed?

In a word, 'no'. Sexual harassment is dependent on the combined effect of two forms of power: individual (or personal) power, and institutional power. As such, sexual harassment cannot be perpetrated by a woman, and although she may have individual power over particular men her power does not have the traditional attitudes and mores of this society supporting and condoning her behaviour. Therefore any sexist behaviour perpetrated by a woman towards a man, whilst embarrassing, humiliating and unwanted, cannot and does not have the same degree of authority as sexual harassment.

Sexual harassment perpetrated by a man can result in a situation which is coercive, frightening, may escalate into sexual assault or even rape, and may have long-term physical, psychological and economic consequences. This is not to say that men are not subject to any kind of sexism or general harassment (this will be dealt with in Chapter 2).

What sexual harassment is not

Sexual harassment is not consensual sexual behaviour between two people who are attracted to each other. It is not flirting, sexual horseplay, sexual games, sexual innuendoes, genuine compliments or touching, hugging, or patting in which both players are happy to engage. People engaged in consensual sexual behaviour are not trying to put one another down. There is no power imbalance; there is no intimidation involved; there is no coercion, fear of reprisals or detriment to one of the participants. As many people first meet their sexual partner in the workplace it is important that a clear distinction be made between sexual harassment and consensual sexual interchange. Sexual harassers do not marry or form loving relationships with the people they sexually harass. Recipients of sexual harassment are not attracted to the perpetrators of such behaviour.

However, it is important to remember that consensual sexual interchange may constitute unprofessional conduct, and be seen as embarrassing if the two people concerned are explicit in their actions and feelings for each other. Consensual sexual conduct within the work or school environment and within work time which affects other workers or students is neither professional nor appropriate. How people feel for each other, expressed through intimate and consensual relationships, should not form part of the general workplace environment.

What women and men see as sexual harassment are often two very different behaviours. If a woman or girl believes that she has been sexually harassed then the complaint must be taken seriously. Just because a man or boy says that he thought she liked it is no indication that his perspective is accurate. Sexual harassment is not based on intentionality.

Discussion

A judge said of women and girls:

'Human experience in the court has shown that women and girls, for all sorts of reasons and sometimes for no reason at all, tell a false story which is extremely easy to fabricate but extremely difficult to refute.'

J. Hopkins (1984, p.81).

Can boys sexually harass women teachers?

The answer to this is clearly 'yes' although how it can come about may be difficult to see at first. I have talked about sexual harassment being dependent on both institutional and individual power and how it is the combination of these two which provides the ingredients necessary to harass.

Whilst it is clear to see how men in more powerful positions can harass, a woman teacher is sometimes puzzled when she feels harassed by one of her pupils. It is because of the power and privilege invested in males which provides the climate for boys to try out their male domination. Whilst it may well be rebuffed by the teacher, it is nonetheless an unwanted intrusion and constitutes sexual harassment.

Miss Manders was an adult recipient of sexual harassment by two boys who were clearly testing out their male supremacy. Two 11 year-old boys, who had been disruptive all year, began to use tactics of sexual harassment towards the end of July. Their behaviour culminated in placing a girl's bra on her desk, with a note saying that it had been found in a male teacher's car. The implication was that Miss Manders and he had been together the previous night. Miss Manders reacted by placing the article in the waste-paper-bin and ignoring it.

Two weeks later the boys put an unused but open condom on her desk with a note, purportedly from the same male teacher, suggesting how Miss Manders and he might use it. At this she got angry. She shouted at the students, and when this got no response, burst into tears and ran from the room.

She asked for help and support from the staff and the headteacher, in particular. Most saw the incident as one in which the 'boys were being boys', and that she had mishandled the first instance. When she insisted that something should be done, the staff began to blame her more vigorously, in particular for trying to keep the students on too tight a rein all year and not realising that they were growing up.

The conclusion to this episode was that Miss Manders, as a direct result of this sexual harassment was asked by the head to take a class of younger students the following year. As she saw this as a criticism of her teaching and as a loss of confidence in her, she left the school.

Thus it can be seen that sexual harassment can be perpetrated by younger boys on older women. Women teachers have also talked about being 'handled' as they go through crowded school corridors, whistled at, and of finding soft porn being looked over by male students.

The consequences of sexual harassment

Sexual harassment is intimidating, embarrassing, humiliating and frightening. The person on whom the sexual harassment is being perpetrated feels that she has no power to stop it, that she cannot necessarily predict when the next attack will come, that no one will believe her if she complains, that there are often no other witnesses to support her account, that if she complains she will be told that she has no sense of humour, that she may get physically hurt next time, that she will be blamed for being provocative, that she is the only one to whom this behaviour is occurring and that if she complains in some way she 'asked' for it. It is for these reasons that many girls and young women remain silent and make no complaint.

Sexual harassment has a number of consequences, which can be classified as primary and secondary. The primary consequences are those that occur in the short term. They may include: staying away from school, skipping particular lessons, becoming silent for fear of further harassment, thinking more about the next attack than the work in hand, losing interest in the particular lesson in which the harassment occurs, avoiding particular places in the school, walking home a different route and isolating oneself from friends. The person being harassed may have headaches, feel depressed, fall behind in her school work, lack concentration, become irritable, and feel stressed and tense.

The secondary consequences can have long-term effects. They include a lack of self-esteem, confidence and diminished self-image. These have an effect on how the girl sees herself succeeding in school and may curtail her career chances. If she has been absent from school, lacked concentration in lessons, and fallen behind in her school work as a result of sexually harassing behaviour, she may be in jeopardy of failing exams and losing the chance to go on to higher or further education.

If she has complained and has been labelled as a trouble-maker, provocateur, liar or a person lacking in the ability to take a joke, this may affect her final report. These consequences may in the long term have economic ramifications, for she may be restricted in her career promotion because of a lack of qualifications.

However, there are medical consequences too. People who are harassed suffer from stress symptoms. Stress is caused by having to cope with unwanted sexual attention, unrelenting anxiety and frustration caused by the harasser's behaviour. Stress can also arise as a result of a complaint having been made, or the effects of putting up with the continual harassment. Stress-related illnesses affect one's feeling of wellbeing, both emotionally and physically. These illnesses may include: depression, tiredness, ulcers, nausea, dependency on mood-altering substances such as tobacco, alcohol or drugs, or heart, nerve or stomach disorders. Finally, family life will be affected if the person who is harassed is uncooperative, moody, irritable and isolated.

CHAPTER 2

Why Sexual Harassment Continues

Introduction

This chapter discusses how sexual harassment is perpetuated and maintained. Within the text are more boxes which can be used in conjunction with educational programmes, rather than as one-off activities. Other forms of unwanted attention to do with the misuse and abuse of power are also discussed.

In what ways is sexual harassment perpetuated?

Sexual harassment exists, and indeed thrives, because of two major features of our society; sex-stereotyping and sexual discrimination. I shall take these two issues separately.

Stereotyping

Boys are encouraged throughout childhood to be independent, aggressive and adventurous, to be leaders, to be boisterous, to be energetic and enthusiastic, to develop physical prowess, business and administrative skills and to have the ability to deal with crises. These messages come from many sources: the media, parents, family friends, teachers, literature, peers, grandparents and other family members.

Discussion
Video about 20 minutes of television advertisements.
Watch them.
In single-sex groups discuss:
In what roles are women portrayed? What do women advertise?
In what roles are men portrayed? What do men advertise?
Do a similar task but use magazines or look at the billboards in your town.

Similarly, girls are encouraged to assume particular roles but these are ones which are nurturing, caring, submissive and emotional. They are taught and encouraged to pay attention to appearances and to have, as a primary interest, domestic rather than world events. It is not considered important that girls have physical or psychological strength, stamina or ambition. Indeed, in acquiring such characteristics girls lose personal power. The activity/passivity divide is often supported in the home with children being given presents which reflect this stereotyping. It is often portrayed that girls sit and read, colour-in, paint, and play with dolls, whilst boys play outside with footballs, cricket balls and war games.

© *Jacky Fleming, reproduced by permission of Penguin Books: London*

This stereotyping is greatly exaggerated by the media where advertisements for children's toys are categorised into those which are suitable for boys and those which are suitable for girls. Watch the Christmas advertisements for toys on the television. Games are devised, advertised and sold on the assumption that boys are active and girls are passive.

Discussion
Make a list of some children's toys.
Why do you think they are advertised as being suitable for either girls or boys?
Is it true that boys can't or shouldn't play with dolls?
Is it true that girls can't or shouldn't play with train sets?

When individual children step outside their gender stereotype the culture around them influences them and encourages them to conform. Thus boys who choose to be passive are labelled 'sissies', 'wimps' and 'girls', and girls who choose to play actively, to climb trees, to be assertive and like outdoor games are called 'tomboys'. Interestingly, our society is far more tolerant of girls being tomboys than of boys dressing up in their mother's high heeled shoes and make-up.

Research
One researcher suggests to borrow a baby (and one of its parents) and take it out into the street and to stop the first 20 people. Tell them you are conducting an experiment to find out how people react to babies. Ask them to hold 'Mark' and tell you what sort of baby they think he is. Repeat with another 20 people but this time ask them what they think of 'Mary' The baby will be the same one in each case. (You may like to dress the baby in more traditionally gender-appropriate clothes such as blue for Mark and pink for Mary). Write down the responses you get.

Discrimination

Discrimination is the act of making a distinction or distinguishing one thing from another. In the context of gender stereotyping, discrimination means the favouring of a particular group for no other reason than one of sex. Sexual discrimination is the direct and indirect favouring of boys and men over girls and women.

Distinction in itself is not discrimination, for everyone is an individual and has different needs. Therefore, as long as the notion of distinction is limited to paying equal but different attention to individuals, it does not constitute discrimination.

Distinction becomes discrimination if people are favoured for no other reason than one of sex, colour, race, religious beliefs or disability.

Discussion

The Sex Discrimination Act 1975 makes discrimination against women or men on the grounds of sex, unlawful in a variety of situations.

The Act defines two sorts of discrimination: direct and indirect.

Direct discrimination against a woman occurs when an employer treats her less favourably than a man because she is a woman.

Indirect discrimination occurs when an employer applies a condition to a woman which applies, or would apply, equally to a man, but:

is such that the proportion of women who can comply with it is considerably smaller than the proportion of men who can comply with it.

it is to the detriment of the woman in question because she cannot comply with it.

it cannot be shown by the employer to be justifiable, irrespective of the sex of the person to whom it is applied.

(Adapted from *The Equal Opportunities Book* by Jim Read, 1988, p.26).

<u>Aim</u>: for students to understand the Sex Discrimination Act and its application.

In our culture, sex discrimination begins at birth and babies are treated differently because of their sex. Research shows that parents' and adults' behaviour towards babies and children is very much influenced by the sex of the baby. There seems to be no such thing as 'sex-neutral behaviour'.

Discrimination occurs at many levels and in many ways. One example of sex discrimination against women, which is clearly identifiable, is in the area of sport activities. Discrimination here in many cases leads to women not participating in sporting events, thus creating a stereotype that women don't like or are not good at sports. Let's look at the way in which sporting events are presented to the community via the media. Much television transmission at weekends covers sporting fixtures. Of the main ones covered, football, horse racing, rugger, cricket, snooker and golf, one would get the impression that it is only men who engage in leisure time physical activity. This image of the athletic male is supported in the home. Often the only one of the partnership who has time to play squash, football, rugger or golf is the man. For many adult women the burden of home management takes up any leisure time they may have. These images on television and the reality in the home are seen and absorbed by children.

Schools too encourage differences to emerge and to be exaggerated. Children in junior and infant schools often divide into male and female playing groups, the boys physically active at playtime whilst many of the girls are less active, preferring to talk and play differently. Whilst girls are acquiring more inter-personal skills, boys develop more athletic characteristics: characteristics which are given more status and reward.

Research

Make a ground-plan of the school playing areas. Plot the areas in which the girls and boys play. Do the same in a junior school classroom, or the science laboratory. What are your findings? What implications can be drawn from the findings?
<u>Aim</u>: to compare the difference in space taken up by boys and girls.

Boys play rugger, football and cricket, games which are played over a large area of ground. Girls, on the other hand, classically play netball and tennis, games which teach body control because of the limited space on the court. Where some teachers do encourage girls to play football during school time, this is not supported by the media or the popular image of football players. Interestingly, boys are seldom invited to learn to play netball. This activity divide, then, is seen as a natural or normal phenomenon and it becomes a self-fulfilling prophesy that girls are naturally more passive than boys, have more control over their bodies, are not active every minute but wait to share, and therefore are able to withstand boredom.

There are some resources in schools which are discriminatory in the material they contain. For example, some reading schemes, used in infant and junior schools, are clearly gender-stereotyped. In *Ginn 360*, a scheme designed in the 1980s, men or boys occur in nineteen active occupations including such roles as an inventor, a demolition crane driver, a helicopter pilot and a forester. Women or girls, on the other hand, are represented in just six roles, half of these in the traditional home environment, washing clothes, preparing food and doing housework. This reading scheme is by no means alone in its gender bias. Research by Rosemary Stones (1983), has shown that children's books have an important part to play in the way children view themselves as males or females and in how they subsequently view themselves as adults. Whilst books of this nature are read by a large proportion of children in schools it is clear that issues of equal opportunity will be harder to address.

The discrimination which has been systematically applied to girls throughout their childhood, education and adolescence has a direct result on how women perceive themselves as adults and in particular how they perceive themselves as workers. However, it is not only women who curtail their own potential, but social pressures and myths. For example, because it is thought that women are better than men in controlling themselves physically, it is believed that they are therefore more suited to inactive work.

This leads to the assumption that they are good at fiddly, repetitive, high concentration tasks, such as technical and electronic assembly work, usually poorly paid and an uncertain job with few promotional prospects. However, if it were true that smaller fingers and better concentration were important for such exacting work then it would seem reasonable to suggest that women should be employed as brain or heart surgeons. Both these high paying and high status jobs are monopolised by men.

The discrimination towards women in sporting events is characteristic of many other areas of life. Employment opportunities, career prospects, and higher education opportunities carry with them similar myths and stereotypes. The effect on women is obvious. Without financial backing, personal support and adequate role-models women are still disadvantaged in the workplace.

Discussion
Name three men and three women:
sports people
television news presenters
television chat show presenters
politicians
scientists
authors
playwrights

From sexual discrimination to sexual harassment

Once men and women reach adulthood they have both experienced the effects of discrimination, but from different perspectives. Women have learned that in the face of individual and institutional male power they lack authority, autonomy and status. This puts them in a disadvantaged position. Similarly, men have learned, often subconsciously, that what they say, what they do and what they want to do are taken more seriously. They are in a position where their authority and autonomy are supported. It is my contention that both parties understand the behaviours which constitute sexual harassment (although they may not know that term). Men use behaviour which is sexually harassing and they have learned this from the way men are portrayed in our society. They have seen other men 'do it' to women. Even if they choose not to use their advantage they implicitly hold this potential. Women, on the other hand, experience sexual harassment as something done to them or other women. Women do not learn how to sexually harass and men do not see other men being sexually harassed by women. By the time boys and girls are adults they have acquired sufficient of the culture's sexist traditions to conform. Discriminatory practices lead to an unequal society. This inequality provides the bedrock on which sexual harassment thrives and exists.

Sexual harassment, like discrimination, begins when children are very young. It is not unique to adults and the workplace. Sexual harassment changes in its nature and form as people grow up and often becomes more subtle and insidious the older the harasser is. Adults are often tolerant of overt sexual harassment by boys, dismissing their actions or considering them to be natural male behaviours. Fundamentally, however, junior school examples of sexual harassment are based on the same principles as the adult version: for the harasser it is the misuse of power, threatening behaviour and coercion: for the recipient it is the fear of reprisals, embarrassment, trivialisation and humiliation and the fear of being thought provocative.

Discussion

It was reported by O'Brien that a male teacher passed a female student a love letter in an O-Level English exam. When she informed the headteacher he said that, 'a young woman of your age should be flattered'.

The Guardian (16th February 1988, p.16).

Sexual harassment occurs in the infant school playground and in the classroom. Boys chase girls around and demand that, if caught, they kiss them. Some boys, in the infant section of a Cambridge private school, played a daily game of chasing the girls around the extensive grounds, singling one out, surrounding her and trying to remove her pants. Jane talked of her experiences in the junior section of a Suffolk school. 'Some of the boys creep up behind us and they just lift up our skirts. They then say, "Oh dear, I'm sorry, I made a mistake". I just hit them and walk away. And sometimes we are going to the loo and sometimes they peep in'.

All of these 'games' constitute sexual harassment if the game is not a game that all the participants want to play and those who are the recipients are embarrassed and threatened. The situation is further exacerbated if the girls complain and their complaint is not taken seriously and nothing is done, thus seemingly condoning the behaviour of the boys as being acceptable, and trivialising the girls' protest.

Drama

In a group act out a well-known fairy story, changing the characters from females into males. Thus Cinderella and Snow White become male, whilst Prince Charming and the Dwarves become female. Show your play to the rest of the class.

Direct sexual harassment

Sexual harassment can occur directly or indirectly. Direct sexual harassment refers to the perpetrator deliberately aiming unwanted attention towards a girl or a group of girls. It encompasses all forms of unwanted attention such as being touched, having hands or rulers put up skirts, being propositioned, being continually asked out on dates, having bra straps 'pinged', being called names or having parts of the body referred to, or references being made to menstruation. Sexual harassment also refers to patriarchal behaviours which coerce girls to conform in certain ways. 'Sexy legs', 'dumb blonde', 'bimbo', and wolf-whistling, whilst not all involving touch or sexual innuendoes, confine girls to behaving in ways which boys, in collusion with societal traditions, think are appropriate for 'young ladies'. These behaviours, for the most part, are ignored by staff and students because they are so frequent, happen when students are unsupervised and because they are usually regarded as normal male behaviour. Further, girls are often reluctant to complain if there is no reliable grievance procedure in the school for this can result in being labelled 'trouble-maker', 'provocative', 'man-hater' and other such unpleasant names.

Discussion
In single-sex groups write down all the derogatory names you can think of to describe women or girls. Do the same for men. What do you find?

Indirect sexual harassment

Whilst direct sexual harassment happens in frequent measure, indirect sexual harassment is endemic in schools. This term refers to the behaviours described above being witnessed by other girls in the class, stairwell or playground. If, as a girl, you witness a female colleague being sexually harassed, you learn indirectly what sexual harassment feels like. To hear girls being called 'slag' or 'slut', to watch another girl being 'felt-up' by a group of boys, to see another girl's tampons or pads being thrown around the classroom, to witness a group of boys trying to remove another girl's jeans, constitutes indirect sexual harassment. Indirect sexual harassment also occurs in graffiti and other visual displays. Pin-ups, sexual diagrams scrawled on walls, text books and desks lead girls to see themselves as sexual objects open to male scrutiny and appraisal. If girls are reluctant to complain about overt sexual harassment they are even less likely to make a complaint about indirect sexual harassment.

Other forms of harassment

Homosexual harassment

Sexual harassment of women by men could, more accurately, be called 'heterosexual harassment'. Homosexual harassment is, as the name suggests, to do with sexual harassment between homosexuals or when one person is a homosexual. Gay men and women are subject to harassment of a sexual nature because other people believe that they, as heterosexuals, are 'better' than them. This is an abuse of power and is based on learned ideas about the nature of sexuality embedded in our culture. Sometimes homosexual harassment is to do with the attitudes and values of the harasser who believes that the homosexual person is wrong in his or her sexual proclivities.

Through harassment the straight person wishes to degrade, humiliate, threaten, embarrass or intimidate the gay person.

Sometimes a gay person sexually harasses a straight person, sometimes a gay person is sexually harassed by a straight person, and sometimes a gay person is sexually harassed by a gay person. Whatever the combination there are commonalities with sexual harassment described in the previous chapter.

As the society in which we live is patriarchal, so too is it heterosexist. Heterosexist means that we live in a society dominated by a heterosexual attitude to life, and homosexuals are oppressed. Heterosexuals make the assumption that heterosexuality is the norm and they maintain their supposed right by dominating. One of the ways in which this heterosexism is manifested is through homosexual harassment.

Bullying

Bullying again is the use and misuse of power, based on an inequality of strength, height, numbers or age. One does not see a smaller, shorter, younger, weaker person alone bullying an older, larger group of people. Again it is to do with power and again bullying succeeds in threatening, humiliating, intimidating, and degrading someone or a group of people. This term I reserve for those people who bully people in a way that is in no way connected with sexual inequality. Bullying occurs between people of the same sex, one man bullying another man, or a group of men bullying one man. This can also happen with women.

Discussion
Imagine a friend of yours is being bullied.
Think of some safe strategies to help them.
Discuss your ideas with others in a group.

The person who is bullied, like the person who is sexually harassed, feels powerless, that there is nothing that can be done, and if they do 'tell' there will be repercussions. Unlike sexual harassment, this behaviour is not considered normal or natural, although many adults ignore children bullying each other, feeling that children have to learn to 'stand on their own two feet'. Bullying, like sexual harassment, can have similar consequences for the victim, such as physical symptoms of nausea, headaches, and tension and other stress-related problems.

Sexual hassle

Sexual hassle is a label I use to describe a particular kind of unwanted sexual attention shown by a woman or girl to a man or boy. There is an important distinction to be made here. Two researchers, Dziech and Weiner, conducted surveys on a university campus in America and discovered sexual attention in the form of unwanted sexual overtures and flirtations shown by female students towards their male professors. Although this behaviour is clearly unwanted, unreciprocated, unsolicited and sexual in nature and meets some of the criteria of sexual harassment there are fundamental differences too. The primary difference is that female students do not have the socially-constructed or institutional power of birthright or patriarchy, for whatever power they do have is held individually and is not collectively organised. 'There is too much difference in role and status of male faculty and female students to make flirtation or even seduction by students harassment. "Harassment" suggests misuse of power and students simply do not have enough power to harass' (Dziech and Weiner, 1984, p.24). While this annoying behaviour might be uncomfortable and embarrassing, this 'crush' is in an entirely different category from sexual harassment, for it cannot destroy self-esteem or endanger intellectual self-confidence. There is no threat for the professor of retaliation in the form of withheld recommendations, punitive treatment or fear of getting unfair low grades. Ultimately the professor has the power to control the situation, whatever the consequences, because of the inherited individual and institutional power bequeathed the male gender.

Sexual hassle, I would say, is becoming more prevalent in our schools in Britain. As girls and young women become more assertive about their role as females, so they, like the boys, try to embarrass and annoy boys or men. In one school in Cambridgeshire, a group of year-eleven girls were found by the deputy head leaning out of the window, making sexist comments to a group of builders working in the school. Whilst the men may have found the treatment embarrassing and humiliating, it cannot be compared to the sexual harassment of girls or women, for two important reasons. Firstly, these girls, as Dziech and Weiner would say, simply do not have enough power to harass. As I have said, sexual harassment is dependent on two forms of power, individual and institutional. Whilst on their own home territory these girls may have stolen some individual power, (even though they are only 15 years old) for a matter of a few minutes, it is impossible to think that, given a different and less safe location, these girls would be in a position to threaten this group of grown men again. Secondly, whilst women and girls may fear that sexual harassment could escalate and ultimately end in rape, men experiencing sexual hassle carry with them neither the dread, nor the potential and inherent intimidation of this ultimate violation.

Sexual harassment is a strategy used exclusively by those with access to the privilege of institutional and individual power, and for this reason males (other than gay men and boys), are free from sexual harassment.

Sexist harassment

I use the term sexist harassment to mean the use of stereotyped preconceptions as to what are appropriate behaviours, attitudes and language for particular genders. It is important that sexual harassment is not seen as a catch-all phrase for all sexist and unwanted behaviour, for this destroys the specific nature of sexual harassment. Sue Wise and Liz Stanley (1987) in their book *Georgie Porgie: Sexual Harassment in Everyday Life*, make no distinction between sexist male behaviour, bullying and sexual harassment.

> 'Elsie Marley was watching the last episode of a thriller on TV - soon she would know "who dunnit". Her dad then came in and said he'd had an awful day, he was ever so miserable and needed cheering up - could they have a nice cup of tea and a good chat? She said he'd have to wait, she was watching something on the telly. He said that sometimes she was really very selfish and then he turned the TV off. When she got up to put it back on again he prevented her, saying that all this was a good laugh wasn't it' (Wise and Stanley 1987, p.4).

In Wise's and Stanley's opinion this is sexual harassment because it involves unwanted and intrusive male behaviour, of whatever kind, forced on a female. Their definition incorporates demands for time, attention and sympathy and for them these are essential features of sexual harassment.

In my opinion this behaviour by Elsie's Dad is sexist harassment. Because he believes, presumably, that a woman's role is to provide tea and sympathy, he has demanded that Elsie provide both. He thinks at an intrinsic level that women are inherently better at these tasks than men. This is sexist harassment rather than sexual harassment because it comes from a stereotyped belief about what constitutes male and female behaviour.

Sexist harassment can affect both men and women and can be perpetrated by either, too. Thus a woman who has a flat tyre and assumes, and expects, a man to change it, is making a similar assumption about the inherent skills and interests of men *per se*. To categorise different activities as male or female is understandable because of the sexist roles ascribed men and women in our society. For example, it is because of the way men have been brought up, and the skills they learn because they are men, that they will be better at changing tyres than women. However, this is not a biological feature of their makeup, it is a learned skill. Thus to ask a man to change a tyre because it is assumed that he will be better at it, or to ask a woman to make a cup of tea and listen to a man's problems because she is somehow born with these skills, is to make assumptions about what men and women like doing and are good at.

If we are to circumvent sexist harassment it is important that we do not make such assumptions about people's individual skills and interests. Further, it is also necessary that we ourselves do not trade on these assumptions and reinforce sexist harassment. Thus it is as inappropriate to make comments about men's inability to be domestic, care for children and knit, as it is to make assumptions about women's ability in car maintenance.

Racial harassment

Racial harassment is defined as hostile or offensive behaviour by a person of one racial or ethnic group against a person of another. As with sexual harassment, behaviour which falls into this category is wide and can encompass such things as name-calling, insults, graffiti, verbal abuse, physical assault or attacks on a person or their property, ridicule, racist jokes, religious or anti-religious comments, innuendoes, racist songs or rhymes. Racial harassment and racism are endemic in our society, and as such are reproduced and maintained in the schooling system. Racial harassment relies on the combination of the two kinds of power already discussed, institutional and individual power, inherent in white individuals and Western institutions.

The Swann Report (HMSO 1985), emphasised how severe forms of racial harassment could result in psychological damage:

> 'We believe the essential difference between racist name calling and other forms of name calling is that whereas the latter may be related only to the individual characteristics of the child, the former is reference not only to the child but by extension to their family and indeed more broadly their ethnic community as a whole'.

Racial harassment can be both direct and indirect. Indirect racial harassment may not be aimed at a person but involves the use of racist behaviour which others might witness. This can occur in an all-white environment.   Examples might be a remark such as 'the black spot in the school' or sayings such as 'to work like a black'. Racial harassment occurs both in social arenas, such as the street, pubs and at parties, and at school and other education settings. If an intimidating or hostile environment is created or perpetuated by a person or a group of people, regarding racial prejudice, this constitutes racial harassment too. The comments or expressions used may not be intentional on the part of the harasser, but they are racist if they are taken to be insulting or offensive.

What supports the continuation of sexual harassment?

Sexism

According to the Commission for Racial Equality (CRE 1987) sexism is 'the pervasive mistreatment of women by men and society as a whole'. It was a term coined by the feminist movement of the 1960s, probably copied from the word racism. These two words reflected the rising awareness of women (and Blacks) of the oppression suffered in our culture by those who were not white males.

It is defined as behaviour, or policy, or language or prejudice, or any other action by men or women which expresses the institutionalised, systematic, comprehensive, or consistent view that women are inferior or can be treated in an inferior way. It is based on the stereotypical view of masculine and feminine roles. Sexism limits women's and girls' options and subjects them to discrimination, exploitation and demeaning treatment on the basis of their sex. Because sexism is often unconscious it is extremely difficult to see or distinguish from what is considered normal human behaviour. However, because it is learned it can be eliminated.

Conundrum

A son and his father are involved in a very bad car accident and the father is killed. An ambulance takes his body to the nearest mortuary. The little boy, although extremely badly injured, is still alive and is rushed by ambulance to the nearest hospital. Emergency procedures ensure that the staff waste no time in getting the boy to the operating table. The surgeon walks in to begin the operation, takes one look at the patient and says, 'I can't operate on this child, he's my son'.
Can you explain this puzzling story?

Sexist language

According to the Commission for Racial Equality (CRE 1987), sexist language is the 'use of language which accepts the male role as the norm and reinforces the female role as secondary and therefore inferior'. Sexist language is the portrayal of male dominance in both language structure and language usage.

Discussion

'A child is, by definition, either male or female. Fashionable though it is to write, talk and behave as if we were all "persons", our sexes are clearly identified by language. We cannot roll a boy and a girl together and call the product "it". Neither can we escape the problem with apparently neutral words like "baby" because as soon as possessive pro-nouns are needed, sentences like "get the baby out of his/her cot and put him/her into his/her chair..." begin to litter the page. So even though this book is about the development, handling, feelings, thoughts and activities of all normal babies, the narrative baby has to be either "he" or "she". I have chosen to use "he" because, even today, it is easier for most parents to accept that pronoun as applying to either sex. Where gender specifically affects a child's nature or needs, you will find a boy or a girl specified'.
Penelope Leach (1979, p.24).

It is a subject which is hotly debated by many people, especially men, who view the eradication of terms, words and phrases which some people think are sexist, as hitting at the heart of language formation and its historical foundations.

However, until there is a systematic eradication of sexist language such as chairman, check-out-girl and businessman, as well as the assumption that surgeon, doctor, scientist and author means men, we are unlikely to move very fast or comprehensively towards equal opportunities and an end to sexual discrimination.

Discussion
In single sex groups discuss these sexist words and phrases:
Manmade
the general use of **he** instead of he and she
the general use of **man** instead of people
She corners well (as a car)
The master bedroom
The office was manned
Mother tongue
Lady Doctor

Domestic violence

Unfortunately, the use of physical violence in families is quite common and is a largely hidden problem. Domestic violence, as it is now called, refers to the abuse of people within the family. Usually the victims of domestic violence are women and children, although women too are responsible for physical violence against children and babies.

The use of physical violence against women is historically based. In England, until the middle of the nineteenth century, wife-beating was assumed to be a normal and acceptable facet of life. Men were legally allowed to beat their wives, if they transgressed their husband's demands, provided the rod or stick was no thicker than a man's thumb.

Proverb
An old English proverb: 'A woman, a dog, and a walnut tree,
The more ye beat them the better they be'.

CHAPTER 3

How Sexual Harassment
is Learned

Introduction

In this third chapter in Section One the theme of institutional and individual power will be continued by looking at how sexual harassment is learned behaviour, rather than a biologically-determined trait. It will be argued that biological differences between men and women are not responsible for sexually harassing behaviour, although there is a common assumption that this is the case. Rather it will be argued that males and females are brought up to behave in different ways because of the gender roles ascribed to people in our society, and that from these gender-based experiences they learn different things about life. One of the different sets of behaviours learned by men is that which constitutes sexual harassment. One of those learned by women is that sexual harassment is an acceptable thing for men to practise. Because men and women see sexual harassment from different perspectives, this means that different messages have been learned by the perpetrator and the recipient. This chapter will look in detail at how the messages have been transmitted and how they come to be used in different ways.

Sexual harassment - a learned phenomenon

The term *sexual harassment* described in Chapter 1, refers to a broad set of unwanted sexual or sexist behaviours, some of which have been acquired during childhood and adolescence. These behaviours are reproduced, learned, maintained and regarded as acceptable by the social institutions in which we live. They are not learned in isolation but as part of our traditional mores, because many of the behaviours which constitute sexual harassment are also those which constitute normal male behaviour. The society in which we live, as already discussed, clearly gives men primacy. It is for two reasons that sexual harassment can exist within this male-dominated society without causing too much concern. First, sexual harassment can be confused with behaviour used by men who are sexually interested in a woman. For example, in their pursuit of partners men and women engage in consensual flirting. The difference between flirting and sexual harassment is solely that the former is mutual, the latter is not. Second, sexual harassment is very similar to other sexist practices, such as patronising behaviour and sexual discrimination. Both these practices are commonly used by men in both professional and personal capacities and as such are institutionalised.

Discussion
Wolf-whistles; are they flattering? Why/why not?

In our society people in more powerful positions often casually touch people with less power, thinking that it is a warm and friendly gesture, whilst people with less power do not feel it is appropriate to initiate touching, patting or any physical contact at all. Because it is men who are mainly in positions of power *vis-à-vis* women, many think it is all right to touch their female colleagues and employees. Many male managers squeeze, pat, stroke and hug their female secretaries. Male teachers sometimes do the same to female students. Often they think that attention of this kind is a friendly gesture, putting the woman or girl at ease, giving her positive feedback and showing her that her work or presence is appreciated. In reality though, it is extremely patronising conduct, for three reasons. Men are making an assumption, first that they have the right to touch women, second, that their touch is wanted and appreciated, and third, that this behaviour only communicates positive feelings. For many women this is not so, for it is an invasion of their private space, an intrusion on their person, it is ambiguous with regards to the quality of their work, and far from communicating a friendly feeling, it communicates distaste and a potential sexual threat.

By the time men and women have reached adulthood, it is likely that both have learned about their roles in society, have learned to copy and reproduce behaviours which are displayed by older people and, moreover, are working within a sexist framework which accepts these behaviours as naturally male or female. At a reasonably young age they internalise what behaviours, gestures and emotions are appropriate to display, because our society encourages boys and girls to conform to their gender-appropriate behaviours. Thus the institutionalised behaviour of sexual harassment is transmitted to the individual man to use or not to use as the case may be.

The ability to be treated unequally can begin before birth. Potential parents often look forward to having children, with preconceived ideas about whether they want a boy or a girl. Grandparents, friends and other relatives all play a part in this pre-baby time too. Comments are made about what the consequences will be for others in the family depending on whether the new baby is a sister or a brother and what he/she will grow up to be, be interested in or inherit, again depending on its sex. Babies' rooms are decorated according to the sex of the child: clothes are bought with its sex in mind. Friends and relatives hold off buying presents or toys until after the birth for then they can buy one which they think is appropriate, depending on whether the child is James or Jane.

Activity
Design a gender-neutral bedroom, toy, play area, wardrobe of clothes or board game for a child.

From the minute babies are born then, they are gendered creatures and are primarily regarded as male or female, rather than 'a human baby', and are treated accordingly. Not only are children treated differently depending on their sex but there are different expectations of behaviour for a child depending on whether it is a girl or boy.

Nursery rhyme
What are little girls made of?
Sugar and spice and all things nice
That's what little girls are made of.
What are little boys made of?
Snips and snails and puppy dog's tails
That's what little boys are made of.

In one study two groups of observers were told to watch the same baby, described to one group as a boy and to the other as a girl. When the baby's behaviour was described by the observers of the supposed 'girl' they saw it as fear, whilst the observers of the supposed 'boy' saw it as anger. Because boys are expected to be brave and courageous their actions are often perceived as this, even when there may well be another and more appropriate explanation. Similarly, a girl's silent reaction to a situation may be interpreted as shyness or non-understanding, when she may have had previous experience and not want to participate.

It seems that adult interpretations of behaviour are also subject to gender bias. In a diary written by a mother of a little girl the different perceptions made by parents of their children's behaviour is noted.

'6 December 1982 (16 months). It is St Nicholas' Day. Four children are together, waiting, two girls and two boys. Although there are only a few weeks' difference in age, the children have reached different stages in their development. Erich is the least bright; he grasps things slowly and is not very sensitive. St Nicholas comes into the room. We adults sing a carol. Three of the children sit quietly and watch what's happening. But not Erich. He's the only one who takes absolutely no notice of what is going on around him and runs about prattling on as before. His little sack of goodies has to be forced on him by his mother. None of the children shows any sign of fear. When it's all over the adults discuss it and Erich's mother says: "Well, my son showed the most spirit. That boy isn't afraid of anything, the way he was running around St Nicholas." I'm amazed at the way Erich's mother ignores the truth. How simply and quickly a boy's mother can interpret lack of comprehension and sensitivity as manliness and strength. In the case of a girl it would have been "She doesn't understand yet"'(Grabrucker, 1988, pp.19-20).

The difference in perception of behaviour also applies to how adult behaviour is described: a man who shouts orders is seen as authoritative and managing, whilst a woman who does the same is considered 'bossy, out of control, or dominating'. A man who cries is considered weak, whilst a woman who cries is considered normal.

Discussion

In April 1981, the South Australian Sex Discrimination Board acknowledged that Ms Gameau had been discriminated against on the basis of her sex in her application for the position of headteacher.

The evidence presented was that looking at cultural stereotypes of sex alone, people who have minimal information about a person other than the sex of the person *assume* other characteristics. If the person is known to be a male, then the stereotype characteristics which are assumed are aggression, assertiveness, problem-solving ability, initiative, decisiveness, unemotionality, interest in worldly matters, dominance, ambition, activity - including energy and enthusiasm, physical prowess and strength, leadership, business ability, and administration and ability to deal with crises.
Similarly, if all that is known is that a person is female, then the characteristics which are assumed are nurturing, caring, submissiveness, low self-esteem, lack of physical and psychological strength, attention to appearance, high verbality and emotionality, low maths/science ability, low problem-solving ability, non-ambition, non-assertiveness and a primary interest in domestic rather than worldly events.
Quoted in Janie Whyld (1983, p.8).

For men to suppress their feelings of sadness and vulnerability, and for women to suppress their authority and autonomy, a learning process has taken place, for each child is born with the potential to feel a range of emotions. Social conditioning has determined which feelings are appropriate for which sex.

Why babies identify with a particular sex has been researched by many people. In some of this research it has been shown that biological features are less important than gender-role expectations in the way in which people acquire masculinity or femininity. John Money conducted research with some hermaphrodites (people whose genitalia are not clearly identifiable as being either male or female). He found that because their parents, hospital staff and the community assigned them a gender they assumed that gender.

At some later stage science made it possible for a 'true' gender typing by chromosome tests. If patients turned out to have a different chromosome result from their 'assigned' gender they found it impossible to exchange gender because of their sex-role stereotyping and personal gender assignment. Thus Money and Hampson concluded that 'the first three years of life set an individual's orientation to gender roles' (in Rapoport *et al.*, 1977, p.192).

Discussion

Think of a time in your childhood when you were told you couldn't do something because of your gender.

What did you do at the time?

Who else was involved?

What did you feel at the time?

What do you feel now?

Share experiences and compare feelings with others in your group.

How men have learned about sexual harassment

As little boys grow up they learn to hide their emotions, be boisterous and adventurous, make decisions, lead, and be aggressive if they want attention. They are taught and they learn to show courage, to bully, to stand up and fight. For this behaviour they have usually had a wide range of role-modelling, ranging from characters on television to other adults around them, from literature to school friends and peers. Their lessons are learned from institutionalised stereotypes.

Boys also get positive feedback from their parents, teachers, relatives and friends for behaving like a 'typical' boy, for being like Daddy and for being a 'man'.

This situation almost looks as if parents and society deliberately set up an 'educational' programme for boys, creating a situation which will inevitably lead to their considering themselves more privileged, more important and, what is more, to have expectations about the way in which they think they should be treated. Clearly this is one of the outcomes of a society which cares more for its sons than its daughters. But is it true of an industrialised Western society that sons are more desired than daughters?

What is clear about the society in which we live is that boys are socially more privileged in every way than girls. Although biologically girls have an advantage over boys in that they are more likely to survive the first few years of life, historically males have always been regarded as more important than females. Indeed, women on the whole are biologically stronger than men in that they are more likely to survive famine, drought and disease, they can withstand more pain and they live longer. However, evidence of the way in which boys are more valued can be seen in numerous customs and traditions created, adopted and maintained within the Western culture.

One of the most severe forms of discrimination is in the area of education. Middle- and upper-class boys have been educated in the sciences, arts, languages and maths for generations. The education that girls of these classes experienced, before compulsory education in 1944, was confined largely to the domestic arts of cooking, sewing and entertaining, with some writing and the learning of foreign languages. Girls as a group were denied academic education until well into the twentieth century although individual girls were tutored in special cases.

Quotation

Jean-Jacques Rousseau, an educationalist of the eighteenth century, often wrote about what girls of that period should learn. He said in one book that a 'woman's education must ... be planned in relation to men. To be pleasing in his sight, to win his respect and love, to train him in childhood, to tend to him in his manhood, to counsel and console, to make his life pleasant and happy, these are the duties of women for all times, and this is what she should be taught when she is young'.

J-J Rousseau (1762, Ch.1).

For working-class boys there were apprenticeships in trades in which there was training to be, for example, carpenters, thatchers, farriers, weavers and spinners. For girls from working-class homes domestic service was one of the few jobs available. When they got married this work ceased.

Even when girls were educated in all subjects alongside boys, a divide became evident. Boys were more likely to take examinations in physics, chemistry and maths whilst girls took examinations in English, biology and French. Whilst more girls pass more examinations than boys, what is significant is that fewer young women go to university than do young men and the subjects and courses taken by these women are not those which have direct or clearly defined pathways into high-salaried, high-prestige and authoritative positions.

Statistics
University Undergraduate Entries (domicile U.K.) in thousands:

Subject	Women	Men
Language-related	20.0	8.5
Social Sciences	16.4	17.9
Multi-discipline	15.7	16.1
Medicine/Dentistry	10.0	11.5
Biological Sciences	9.9	7.8
Humanities	7.5	8.3
Physical Sciences	5.7	15.1
Studies allied to Medicine	4.6	2.3
Mathematical Sciences	3.9	12.0
Business/Financial stds	4.0	6.2
Engineering/Technology	3.6	25.1
Vet. Sci., Agric/ rel'd stds	2.0	2.2
Creative Arts	2.6	1.6
Education	2.8	0.7
Architecture/rel'd stds	1.1	2.5
Library/ Info. Science	0.1	0.1
All Subjects	110.0	138.0

University Statistics, (1989/90) Vol. 1, *Staff and Students*, D.E.S.

In the past, sons of wealthy landowners inherited lands and wealth. Their sisters were found suitable husbands to protect them and keep them. Women could not inherit property in the Victorian age, could not own land, on marriage all their own wealth or property became that of their husbands, and, even the women themselves were considered to be the property of their husbands.

Even today there are remnants of these traditions. Boys are still regarded as more important. They are often more desired by parents and grandparents because it is the males in Western families who carry on the family name or inherit particular family heirlooms, property and wealth. Even the education system of the 1990s provides an inequality of opportunity despite the numerous reforms instituted both formally and informally. The education boys receive is advantaged in comparison with girls of the same class, age and race.

Boys are allowed more freedom socially and sexually and are encouraged to be more active physically. Boys can earn more money as part-time employees, are more likely to be hired as after-school workers, and at school are encouraged more to plan for and expect a career.

Quotation
'The domestic crafts start with a built-in advantage - they are recognizably part of adult living. Girls know that whether they marry early or not, they are likely to find themselves eventually making and running a home; moreover, some quite young schoolgirls, with mothers out at work, are already shouldering considerable responsibilities - a fact which needs to be taken into account in school housecraft programmes'.
Newsom Report, (1963, para. 388).

At an intrinsic level boys and men are seen as the norm, while women and girls are seen, as Simone de Beauvoir calls it, as 'the Other' (1949, p.65). By this I mean, whatever is defined as human as opposed to animal, is represented by the male. Thus a 'normal human' is seen to have attributes of rationality, logicality, independence, ambition, self-sufficiency, adaptability, as well as decision-making abilities, strong beliefs which will be defended, self-reliance and reliability.

Quotation
'One is not born, rather one becomes a woman'
Simone de Beauvoir (1949).

Whilst these attributes are regarded as predominantly human they are also clearly male if one considers, for example, how women are described. Women are seen to have attributes of irrationality, illogicality, unreliability, dependence, to be unambitious, emotionally inclined, not to hold strong beliefs and be reliant on somebody else, usually a man.

Discussion
Dale Spender, educational writer and researcher writes:
'In the classrooms where I have kept a record, not only do girls get less teacher attention, they are required to wait longer.... In general, boys take up more space, even when they are a minority. They take up more space on their chairs (legs frequently extended as obstacles to unwary travellers), their chairs and desks take up more space, they move around the room more.... In the tapes that I have made in the classroom there is evidence that boys frequently make insulting and abusive (often sexually abusive) comments to girls'.
Dale Spender (1982, pp. 61-63).

These beliefs affect the way in which we see people. Because women are often represented as lacking particular characteristics, such as leadership, decision-making and analytical skills, so myths arise that women are not good at or capable of succeeding in jobs in which these skills are needed. Thus fewer women are given research scholarships, electoral seats, ministerial positions, partnerships in law firms or made chairpersons of corporations, or professors of faculties, or chancellors of universities, or judges, or surgeons or bank managers, because of the preconceived ideas and notions about how women should operate, do operate, may behave and should behave.

Quotation

'Men may cook or weave or dress dolls or hunt humming birds but if such activities are appropriate occupations of men, then the whole society, men and women alike, votes them as important. When the same activities are performed by women they are regarded as less important'.

Margaret Mead, (1950).

But how much of this is to do with how society wants its women to be, rather than to do with what women can do? Does our society want women to be independent, self-reliant, decisive, dominant, efficient, analytical, willing to take risks, aggressive, individualistic, competitive and ambitious, and to have strong personalities? Thought, language, traditions, attitudes and value systems and institutional structures are still predominantly male-oriented, giving men and boys a far greater advantage than at first detected.

The advantage for one individual man or boy is not particularly significant on its own. But when most men and boys possess such advantage, it contributes to a significant difference in social status between males and females and gives rise to self-fulfilling prophesies about boys' characteristics. Whilst society believes and acts as though boys are more important and have more worth, boys are likely to expect this as their right. As I see it, with a positive self-image, a better education and with confidence it is more likely that boys will become adults with the feeling that they have a 'right' to behave in certain ways, to expect certain privileges and a belief that they are naturally dominant, naturally more aggressive and naturally the most important.

What is of interest about these dominant behaviours is that they are considered to be 'OK', quite acceptable and, in fact, by some people, important and necessary to acquire if the person is to assume his mantle of natural maleness. What must be understood though, is that these dominant, aggressive and sexual privileges are learned behaviours. Some of the myths we have regarding male sexuality come from the previous century when it was thought that denying men sexual release was dangerous for their health. Women were expected and taught to suppress their own needs and sexual feelings and respond only to their husband's demands.

Discussion

William Acton, (1813-75), a British expert on sex issues writing in the nineteenth century, claimed that if a woman refused her husband sexual relations over a period of time, such as in the case of pregnancy, this would be 'highly detrimental to the health of her husband, particularly if he happened to be strongly sexually disposed'. He continued: 'The more conscientious the husband and the stronger his sexual feelings, the more distressing are the sufferings he is doomed to undergo, ultimately too often ending in impotence'.

Hellerstein *et al.*, (1981, p.179).

Aim: to discuss the ways in which the myth, that men have uncontrollable sexual drives, has developed.

Still today we have vestiges of these beliefs. Thus in a society where these are allowed and encouraged to persist sexual harassment can be reproduced and maintained. This means that sexual harassment as a phenomenon is learned within a context which supports and encourages men and boys to 'sow their wild oats', be sexually aggressive, sexually appraise women and girls and initiate sexual encounters.

Discussion

What do the following sentences mean?

He sowed his wild oats.

Boys will be boys.

A woman's place is in the home.

The boys are on the loose.

That girl is loose.

He's a stud.

She's a slag.

A girl should save herself.

Not all men harass: not all women are recipients

Having said all the above, there is a caveat which must be explored in this chapter. Whilst I have written, and in many respects made assumptions, about *all men and boys* being treated and brought up in particular ways, this is too simplistic an hypothesis to hold much water. I can hear readers saying: 'but my father wasn't like that, my mother made all the important decisions in our house'; 'my brother was extremely shy and nervous as a boy, he still is, he wouldn't say boo to a goose'; 'my son hates sports and has always preferred reading and growing plants'.

What we are discussing here is power: individual and institutional power. I have already described in Chapter 1 the ways in which institutional power exists and have shown how it influences people, confining their individuality and ensuring common adherence to stereotype. When men are individually powerful and this is supported by their position in an institution, which in itself maintains and reproduces male power, men have the potential to be more powerful than women of the same class, race, religion and educational standard.

Discussion

Are these pairs simply male/female variants, or do the different words carry different connotations?

Landlord/landlady

She's a professional/He's a professional.

Master/Mistress

Bachelor/Spinster

Governess/Governor

Sir/Madam

Lady/Lord

Heir/Heiress

Witch/Wizard

Tailor/Seamstress

Squaw/Brave

Of course not all men use or abuse that power. Where do women stand on this? It has been observed by Valerie Walkerdine (1990, p.11) that girls are not oppressed, passive and dominated in all areas of their life, all the time, by all men or boys. This is clearly true. So when we look at girls playing in schools we often see them playing games which are not physically oriented such as football, but those which usually contain a degree of negotiation and discussion.

If we look at these games more closely we can see that the girls often choose those in which women dominate. The aspect of life in which women have a high profile and are prominent is in the home and family. Thus one explanation as to why girls like to play Mummies and Daddies is that in this game they have access to the decision-making role. Acting out being a mother can give girls the opportunity to experiment with authority and control. However, from my research amongst girls who play these games few boys choose to join in. 'Mummies and Daddies' is one way that girls can experiment with power by reproducing, maintaining and practising their authority and decision-making skills in a game notably reserved for the female gender.

So what I am suggesting is that sexual harassment as a concept is kept alive by the stereotypes and images prevalent in our society, rather than in every man using sexually harassing techniques on every woman he meets.

How women have learned about sexual harassment

As men are not born sexual harassers, neither are women born passive recipients of this behaviour who put up with it because that is the 'natural' way to deal with such attention. However, most women take the attitude that the intrusion of sexual harassment in their lives is a fact of life and nothing can be done about it. Classically, women and girls are silent about being sexually harassed. They often feel that it is their responsibility that it happened and that they have in some way been 'provocative' in dress, word, gesture, look or behaviour.

Discussion

'Women who say no do not always mean no. It's not just a question of saying no. It is a question of how she says it, how she shows it and makes it clear. If she doesn't want it, she only has to keep her legs shut and she would not get it without force, and there would be marks of force being used.'

Judge Wild, 1982, quoted in J. Hopkins (1984, p.71).

Girls and women often feel responsible for acts of unwanted sexual attention. The myth exists that men and boys are physically uncontrollable once sexually aroused. If an adolescent boy sees a teenage girl wearing summer clothes, such as a bikini top and shorts, he may believe she is being provocative or sexually promiscuous. More seriously, however, he may think she is 'asking' for it and that he can touch her, wolf-whistle at her or leer. These myths about male sexuality persist into adult life too.

If a woman allows a man to kiss her then denies him any further sexual intimacy and he rapes her out of rage, society is likely to see this act as one of provocation on the part of the woman, as one of understandable frustration on the part of the man and not as an act of rape at all. In this case the woman is deemed responsible for the actions of the men because that is how society often views sexual behaviour. Women and girls are the custodians of society's morality.

Girls have also learned very different ways of behaving, of acting and of talking from boys. Many learn that tears, passivity and emotional outbursts are acceptable as this conduct often elicits a positive response from adults. A little girl finds that to be flirtatious and seductive brings praise and attention. Although many people believe that little girls are 'naturally' provocative, I would suggest that this is not so, rather they have learned very quickly what behaviours are successful and which are not. They have learned these traits partly from how women and girls are portrayed on television as well as from seeing how other females, such as their mother, older sister and grandmother, behave in front of men and the positive responses gained.

© Chrissie Tate, reproduced by permission of Cath Tate Cards: London

Women in advertisements are most often represented in one of two ways. One is that of the young, attractive, sexy, fashionable and vulnerable 'doll', waiting to be rescued, given chocolates or driven to paradise in the latest model car. Her body is used to advertise anything from car batteries to after-shave. The other image is that of the caring and domestic Mum who washes clothes to a super softness, makes sandwiches with wholesome bread and dairy-spread and who can always find the right pain killer for her husband's headache.

However, yet again the image that has been presented is based very much on the belief that women are dominated willingly, that they have no power whatsoever and cannot stand on their own, suggesting that women are miserable victims of circumstance and behaviour. Of course this is not the case. We all know women who are strong, powerful and autonomous.

From sex-role stereotyping to sexual harassment

It seems clear from these arguments that before children become adults they have learned to use a variety of behaviours which can be identified as appropriate for the male or female gender and that they have been encouraged to use them. At an early age children are able to distinguish between boys' behaviour and girls' behaviour and to tell you what is the proper thing for a boy to do and what for a girl. Even when children have mothers or fathers who step outside stereotyped roles with their father being a nurse or home-maker, their mother being a surgeon or a bank manager, children are

c

clear about what is considered normal for others and that Mummies *should* stay at home while Daddies mend the car and go out to work.

Discussion
Make a list of those jobs which you think should be reserved for either one sex or the other? Why?

Intimidating male behaviour of girls can start very young. Even though the perpetrator may be unaware of what he is doing he knows that it is to do with being a male. Thus boys at the age of 5 look up girls' skirts, try and pull down girls' pants and peep into the girls' lavatories at school. Some of these behaviours constitute sexual harassment, for girls find them embarrassing, humiliating and unwanted. At one school, Suzanna told me that the boys had devised a game in which particular girls were surrounded and then a rhyme was chanted

'Hands up
Stick 'em up
Turn around
Skirts up.'

Suzanna said that the choice was either to comply with the rhyme and have the boys look at your knickers and laugh, or to be kissed. 'I hate that', she said.

Girls' behaviour in the face of unwanted sexual attention is interesting. Because of the way in which girls and women have been taught to behave, their unconscious response to sexual harassment is confusing. Girls and women are not taught to be assertive, to say what they want, to argue and to repel such attention. Often in the face of a sexual harasser a girl will giggle, look coy, think the boy wants to be her 'boyfriend', not object to this behaviour but seek protection from the perpetrator, or entertain visions of romance and a wedding by believing that she has been singled out for special treatment because she is desirable or beautiful. On other occasions she may laugh, or when chased, run away screaming. These protests, however, are not taken seriously by adults, rather they are seen as promoting the myth that girls 'play hard to get'.

Knowledge of this sort has been acquired by both sex groups, but from different perspectives. For men, sexual harassment has been learned from the perspective of the 'doer', or having seen other men 'do it' to women. Women, on the other hand, have had the experience of having had it 'done' to them, or having seen 'it done' to other women. Both groups have learned the different skills needed to 'do' sexual harassment or to 'receive' it, according to their gender identity. Women do not learn how to sexually harass men, because this is not a model of behaviour available to them and they do not occupy the necessary power bases. Further, the traditions and mores in our society do not encourage women and girls to be sexual predators or to initiate in sexual matters. Men, on the other hand, have come to realise that they hold a particular position with greater power than women, and that this method of expressing their power is a possible, and often 'appropriate' way of behaving, considering the norms of our society.

© Viv Quillin, reproduced by permission of Cath Tate Cards: London

For women, society has drawn a fine line between respectable and disreputable behaviour, although the line seems to move about and be dependent on a number of wavering variables. To get the balance right is enormously difficult. Women are expected to dress in a sexy but not provocative way; to present themselves attractively but not like a 'tart'; to wear fashionable and feminine clothes and not outlandish or mannish attire; to be flirtatious and attentive to men's needs, but not seductive and sexually promiscuous. The problem is that the effect depends on the observer's interpretation.

One is not born knowing how to sexually harass. A man does not reach adulthood naturally belittling, embarrassing, intimidating or humiliating women, rating them out of ten for their sex appeal, wolf-whistling at them in the street, patting them on the bottom or making sexual innuendoes about them within earshot. Actions, gestures, looks, comments, sighs or grunts which belong in the category of unwanted sexual behaviour are all learned.

Learning to put up with sexual harassment

The prevailing attitude towards sexual harassment, that there is nothing that can be done because 'boys will be boys', is as much a learned behaviour on the part of the girls as the actual behaviour is learned action by boys. Girls often learn during their childhood that sexual harassment or 'flattery' as it is sometimes called, is part of 'their lot' of being a girl and that females are sexual objects to be judged and appraised. Girls are often taught that to be wolf-whistled at is approval, that 'it makes your day' and that they should be pleased. This message totally masks women's and girls' genuine reaction to such behaviour, which is likely to be irritation or embarrassment. At the least girls and women are expected to take this appraisal positively and to be passive in the face of unwanted sexual attention.

The myth that sexual harassment is flattery is an interesting one. Whilst men and boys dictate how particular behaviour will be received, those who choose to describe it as intrusive and unwanted are often labelled as deviant, humourless and 'priggish'. Further, such behaviour on the part of men is extremely hard to deal with. A group of men on a building site a few storeys up are entirely safe from any verbal response or physical reaction a woman might have. Equally, whistles from a passing car, shouts from a bus or a leer from a group of lads in the market square are extremely hard to challenge.

However, there is a difference between believing or labelling this type of behaviour as acceptable or even flattering, and knowing it to be sexual harassment but also being aware that at some levels there is nothing that can be done. Those who believe that sexual harassment is desirable and flattering behaviour, rather than demeaning and intrusive, have learned male and female roles well. They have learned that this kind of male attention is one way in which they will be noticed and that this is certain proof of their femininity. What they do not realise is that they are being appraised as sexual objects, not as people. Sometimes a girl assesses her social success by the number of men or boys who make approving gestures or comments. In this way women are assessed by their looks, their clothes, their passivity, but not according to what they are like as people.

Discussion
A definition of a feminist
'I myself have never been able to find out precisely what feminism is: I only know that people call me a feminist whenever I express sentiments that differentiate me from a doormat ...'. Rebecca West (1913, *The Clarion*, Nov 14).

SECTION TWO

Dealing with Sexual Harassment

CHAPTER 4

Policy Writing

Introduction

The first section of the book has argued that sexual harassment is dependent on two forms of power; institutional and individual. It has been explained how each form of power operates and the ways in which it is maintained and reproduced in successive generations of children has been discussed. Thus it would seem sensible, when addressing the issue of sexual harassment and attempting to eradicate it from society, that we deal with it in precisely the same way as it occurs, through the institutions and individually. The first two chapters in this section look at the way in which sexual harassment can be tackled by writing a policy, as well as introducing aspects of sexual harassment-awareness into the school curriculum. Both of these can seen as institutional initiatives.

Facts
Women constitute half the world's population, perform nearly two-thirds of its work hours, receive one-tenth of the world's income and own less than one-hundredth of the world's property.
United Nations Report, 1980.

Institutional sexual harassment

The most effective way of dealing with sexual harassment in an institution, on a long-term comprehensive level, is to devise, implement and monitor a sexual harassment policy. The National Curriculum states:

> 'In order to make access to the whole curriculum a reality for all pupils, schools need to foster a climate in which equality of opportunity is supported by policy to which the whole school subscribes and in which positive attitudes to gender equality, cultural diversity and special needs of all kinds are actively promoted' (Curriculum Guidance 3, The Whole Curriculum: NCC, 1990, p.3).

Writing a school policy on sexual harassment

A policy on sexual harassment for the school is vitally important if there is a genuine commitment to stop sexually harassing behaviour throughout the institution. As many workers as possible should be involved in the development of such a policy. It is inadvisable that one person writes alone, for a number of reasons.

First, the person who offers to do so is likely to be aware of the issues already and needs no education on the subject, so that the opportunity to provide a good learning experience is missed. Secondly, writing a whole-school community policy can raise the issue to a level where all members of the school community are involved. Third, writing in isolation creates a document owned by one person, which has to be imposed on others. By inviting others to form the policy it can be ensured that it is a whole-school document, not the property of one person. This makes it more likely that each member of staff will feel responsible for its implementation.

Who should be involved?

If sexual harassment is to be stopped systematically, all staff who are involved with students in any way will need to have an understanding of what sexual harassment is and what the school intends to do with students and staff who complain and with the perpetrators of sexual harassment. Even though the behaviour is entrenched in social practices, sexual harassment as a named phenomenon is a relatively new industrial issue. It is recommended that governors, given their role, power and responsibilities under the Education Reform Act 1988, be involved from the very beginning.

Included in any policy must be a training or awareness-raising programme which takes account of the particular roles and needs of teachers, governors, part-time teachers, new staff, new governors, parents, secretaries, school nurses and doctors, dinner personnel, caretakers, bursars and any other full- or part-time, paid or voluntary workers, or student teachers within the school community. In addition, it will be important for visitors to the school to be aware of the policy so that when, for example, guest speakers are invited to speak about particular career options they do not talk or behave in ways that reflect sexual discrimination or sexual harassment. As many people as possible need to be involved because sexual harassment can be found in all areas of the school community: classrooms, play areas, corridors, canteen, staffroom and stairwells. Sexual harassment can also occur on public transport and school buses and during non-school-based activities, such as field trips, camps, outings and work experience.

How to get started

Many people believe that sexual harassment doesn't exist, or, at least, that it is a rare occurrence, and that women are complaining about nothing; many more people misunderstand what it is. One of the statements I most frequently hear is, 'Sexual harassment, I wish I could get some!' (See Appendix 1). Therefore, once an agreement has been made that this issue will be dealt with through a policy document, the next step is to raise the awareness of as many people in the school community as possible. This can be in both formal and informal ways, through workshops, staff meetings and lessons, newsletters to parents, information nights at school, governors' meetings, parent/teacher interviews, and through casual conversations over coffee in the staffroom, or moments in class where an incident of this nature happens. In my experience, eliminating sexual harassment from schools is essentially a matter of revealing the attitudes which underlie such unacceptable behaviour. Devising a school policy which incorporates ethos and curriculum initiatives is the best way of actively challenging these values and attitudes.

The second stage in devising an effective policy is to nominate those people who will be responsible for the writing and drawing up of such a document. Precisely what you do and how you do it will be governed by the particular climate in the school, your position, the commitment of senior management and other competing interests or priorities. It would be unrealistic to believe that everyone will be as committed as you or even that everyone will understand the message. As already stated, senior management should take an active part in the devising and implementing of such a policy, so that it is seen to be an important issue and not one that a group of interested teachers are preparing in isolation. Without such backing it is likely that the policy development and implementation will fail, resulting in the attempt being seen as a trivial innovation by a group of women.

Teachers or students who are being introduced to the concept of sexual harassment for the first time are likely to be questioning and sceptical. Try not to alienate them at the outset. You will need their support if the policy is to be successful. A series of meetings will probably be necessary for you to present the facts, for them to discuss the myths about sexual harassment and clearly understand what it is they are dealing with.   Speeding-up this process will be neither productive nor expedient in the long term if your audience becomes alienated or resentful. Change in attitudes is slow and many difficult questions, negative responses and angry reactions are likely to arise in the process.

There are many ways of introducing the idea that sexual harassment needs to be dealt with in your school community. You might:

- Collect anecdotes about incidents of sexual harassment which happened in your school. Ask students or staff for their experiences. (At this stage it may not be helpful to make a distinction between sexual harassment, homosexual harassment, bullying, sexual hassle and sexist harassment. This can be done at a later stage, when it becomes appropriate).

- Ask a member of a Teachers' Union to talk to you about their Sexual Harassment Policy.

- Employ a consultant or adviser to help you.

- Circulate a general statement about why sexual harassment is important, what the educational consequences might be for some recipients, and why it is necessary to have a school policy.

- Invite a Theatre-in-Education team, who are currently doing a programme on sexual harassment or equal opportunities, to the school.

- Talk informally about the issue to as many people as possible, in particular with senior management.

- Invite people from outside your school who have already been through the process to come to talk and pass on their expertise.

Once a need to write a policy has been identified, it will be necessary to formally organise a working party. As already stated, the wider the representation on the working party the more likely the policy is to be comprehensive and relevant and to be implemented with conviction when the time comes.

Clearly, consideration should be given to times for the working party to meet, whether in school or outside school and, if the meetings are arranged for before or after school, how teachers with family responsibilities are to attend.

Consideration should also be given to the structure and format of the working party. A commitment to adult learning principles should be evident. It is important that the group be encouraged to take responsibility for their learning, the pace of the learning, the product, the implementation process and evaluation of the finished product. All the time it will be important to inform and to keep up-to-date the members of the school community who are not actively involved in this process.

What should the policy say?

The policy statement must clearly and simply state that all workers within the school community have a right to be treated with dignity; that sexual harassment within the school will not be permitted or condoned; that all workers have a right to complain; that every complaint will be taken seriously and that something will be done about their complaint; that sexual harassment denies the rights of the individual; that it can be prevented, or its prevalence or effect reduced, by empowering recipients to oppose it. The policy must also state that victimisation will not be ignored and those found to be victimising people who make complaints will be dealt with severely.

A policy on sexual harassment for the school community could include the following sections:

- What constitutes sexual harassment in this school community? (Consideration must be given to verbal, non-verbal and physical harassment, graffiti, sexually explicit material, flashing and other manifestations of unwanted attention).

- How will different modes of harassment be dealt with: adult to adult; adult to student; student to adult; student to student?

- What training methods will be used to ensure all governors, staff and students understand the policy?

- How is sexually harassing behaviour to be recorded and monitored? What about confidentiality? Who should know: parents, tutor, etc.?

- A list of trained personnel to whom recipients can go when they wish to make a formal/informal complaint.

- Details of how the recipient and perpetrator will be dealt with, including how post-harassment support will be provided. It will be important to stress the underlying rationale that education is preferable to punishment.

- Details of how the efficacy of the policy and the education programmes will be evaluated.

The sexual harassment policy should state that prompt action will be taken as soon as an incident is notified. The action can take various forms, depending on the situation itself and the variation of the harassment. There can be no one way of dealing with cases, for all will be different. As a consequence, when dealing with an incident consideration must be given to:

- the frequency of the harassment

- the ages of the recipient/perpetrator

- the relationship of the perpetrator to the recipient (student to student, adult to student, student to adult)

- the nature of the behaviour

- the place/time of the abuse

- the wishes of the complainant[*].

---

[*]In most cases the decision as to how an incident of sexual harassment will be dealt with will be up to the recipient, unless it is deemed that the behaviour is of such severity that action has to be taken irrespective of their wishes.

Possible setbacks in policy development

Sexual harassment is an emotive issue and it is unlikely that the passage of developing, writing and implementing the policy will be without incident. The major problem will probably be criticism by people who do not see that this is an important or worthwhile initiative. Their feelings about the proposed policy, possibly directed at the instigators, may be expressed in a variety of ways:

- teasing

- trivialisation of the issues/dismissive comments/jokes

- anger or hostility

- silence

- absence

- pedantic criticisms of policy drafts

- criticism of the constitution of the working party.

Those who are likely to bear the brunt of this behaviour are female staff and students. It is important that this be considered within the working party and ways of supporting those people decided upon. Of course, it is ironic that some of the behaviour demonstrated throughout the policy development may well constitute sexual harassment. Also, in my experience, it is often those people who feel least confident about their attitudes and values who argue the fiercest and it is they who most need a 'softly softly' approach.

Now that it's written

Once the school policy is written, it does not mean that everything can be forgotten. In order that the policy be seen to be a living document and one which is to be taken seriously, a number of strategies need to be employed.

• All school personnel, including governors, staff, parents and students, should have access to a copy of the sexual harassment policy. Newcomers will also need copies when they arrive.

• Training should be part of the school's annual programme.

• Sexual harassment should be addressed as a topic within the curriculum.

• Incidents of sexual harassment should be dealt with immediately, whenever they happen in the school.

• The document should be updated and modified as relevant.

• Parents should be made aware of harassment incidents which affect their children.

CHAPTER 5

Curriculum Initiatives

Introduction

Whilst policy writing is an essential step in eradicating sexual harassment from a school community, it will not be effective if students and staff are unaware of the preconditions for sexually harassing behaviour, the reasons for its existence, with whom it happens and why it is perpetrated and maintained. If sexual discrimination, sexism, sexist language and a general disrespect for women and girls occur within the school community, it is unlikely that sexual harassment will cease, or even be seen to be an issue.

Therefore it is extremely important that sexual harassment becomes a topic in the curriculum. Sexual harassment, as we know, does not happen in a vacuum, but as part of an historical, social and educational legacy. These aspects need to be understood by everyone if incidents are to be reduced or even eliminated all together.

Implicit initiatives

Introducing changes at an implicit level, or dealing with the 'hidden curriculum' as it is sometimes called, is an extremely difficult task. I have already argued that sexual harassment does not exist in isolation, but as part of a much broader disparity between men and women within this society. Sexism, sexist behaviour and sexual discrimination are very much part of our social life and it is therefore reasonable to suggest that they are not absent from most school environments. In fact, as schools are microcosms of society it is inevitable that they are sexist, controlled by patriarchal attitudes and places where sexual harassment is actually on the hidden curriculum as a thing for boys to learn how to do, and for girls to learn how to put up with. Because discriminative practices towards women and girls are so firmly entrenched in the culture, and are often regarded as the 'way things are meant to be', being able to see discrimination in order to challenge it is a first major step. Being able to 'see' sexual discrimination and getting others to 'see' it too, is the key to getting people motivated to reflect on, not only the traditions and mores of our society, but essentially on their own attitudes, values and behaviour. There are no easy solutions to this key issue other than to realise that how you get students involved in learning the subject you teach is based on exactly the same principles.

In addition to generalised social inequality, sexism and sexual discrimination happen at all levels of schooling and can be found in, among other things, teaching methods, resourcing policies, promotion prospects, sporting facilities, career counselling and expectations, and management structures.

Some institutional sexism which remains in primary schools is fairly basic stuff and could be changed relatively easily. Of course the first step will be to convince others that the following are sexist and discriminatory. School registers often list children in two separate groups: the boys first followed by the girls or the other way round. There is no reason why this should be continued other than traditionally. Children in primary schools are often lined up in boys' and girls' lines. Why? Have the children line up alphabetically, by birthdays, by the colour of their jumpers, but not by sex. Boys' good behaviour is often rewarded in primary classrooms by allowing them to play with construction kits, Lego and similar stereotyped activities. Girls are, first, less likely to be rewarded for good behaviour (because of the stereotype that girls are better behaved than boys and therefore don't need incentives) and second, if they are rewarded they are more likely to be rewarded with verbal praise. Girls are also more likely to be praised for attractive, neat and well-presented work than boys, who are commended for originality.

Because institutional sexism is so insidious it will be necessary to deal with sexist practices throughout the school community, and every area of the school needs to be considered. Subjects such as Maths[1], Physics[2], Chemistry, General Science[3], Technology, Computer Studies, CDT[4], Domestic Science[5] and Geography[6] can be sexist in the resource material used, in the assumptions that are made as to the competence or level of interest of boys and girls in the subject and in the way in which the subject is actually taught.

Therefore it is essential for teachers to deal with sexism found within these areas whenever they come across it. Drawing students' attention to the fact that many text books omit women's achievements, use the pronoun 'he' or the word 'man' when referring to men and women, give exercises which focus on the male world, as well as the general problem of boys' domination of resources, air-space and teachers' time, is necessary and will make a significant contribution to ensuring this issue is being dealt with on a broad front.

One way of hearing what boys and girls think and feel about different aspects of sexism, inequality or sexual harassment is to put them in single-sex groups (see p.66). This will avoid the problem of participants being contradicted by students of the opposite sex who do not understand their specific concerns. Single-sex groups also give the students the chance to learn skills which are difficult to learn in mixed groups because of the way they often operate. Because boys tend to dominate air-space, decide on discussion topics and take control of the group, it is important that girls learn and practise the skills of chairing, leading discussions, actively contributing and making decisions. Equally, too, it is important for boys to learn to share time, to negotiate effectively, to be more democratic and to listen to each other's contribution.

At a wider level, if a school's management structure is male-dominated, it may be necessary to consider the promotion policy, the advertising and recruitment method or the general climate within the school which encourages or discourages women to stay or resign. Meeting times, meeting procedures or policy documents may also need to be scrutinised with a non-sexist eye.

Because sexual harassment as a phenomenon is not a natural way of behaving it is possible to look at ways in which the underlying principles and beliefs which maintain and perpetuate it can be challenged, and new ways of behaving, thinking and responding found. Mutual respect for each other is an important step in gaining equality, whilst improving skills of communication is one way of achieving this aim.

Dealing with sexual harassment at an explicit level is to address it directly as part of the planned curriculum in subject areas where it fits reasonably. Personal and Social Education[7], English Literature, English Language[8], Religious Studies, Drama[9], History[10], and Social Studies are all such subjects which could incorporate aspects of this topic (see also Appendix 2).

Sexual harassment, as already shown, is perpetuated and maintained because of the unequal distribution of power between men and women in our society. This inequality has to be addressed and can be, in many ways, in different subject areas. For example, putting women into history changes the perception that this subject is solely about the exploits, conquests, adventures, advancements, and discoveries of men[11]. Asking questions about what women were doing in prehistoric, Roman, Anglo-Saxon, Tudor, Stuart[12], Queen Anne, Victorian, and Edwardian times[13], is important in order that girls realise that women's history has largely been omitted, ignored or not written down and therefore much of it is lost. However, it is also important that women are not merely added as a token gesture and their contribution judged against the contributions of men, but that care is taken to reinterpret women's roles from a woman-centred point of view, otherwise the opportunity to study women, 'on their own terms', will be missed[14].

English Literature is a subject which is teeming with examples of women's financial, social and educational disadvantage. Once a non-sexist eye has been developed, it is possible to pick out pieces of text which would be suitable for discussion with students regarding the place of women in society. Whether the level is early primary education and the piece of literature a nursery rhyme (see Appendix 2), or middle juniors reading Roald Dahl's *The Witches,* or sixth form students studying Thomas Hardy's *Tess of the d'Urbervilles,* the way in which women are portrayed gives ample scope for comparisons with other literary characters and discussions of the role of women today.

Take, for example, the journey that Tess is forced to make with Alec d'Urberville (see Appendix 2). Unless she allows him to kiss her he threatens to drive the horse-cart fast and dangerously to frighten her. Because he is in a position of power, financially, socially and educationally and he is the son of her employer, she is not in a position to complain. What is this but sexual harassment?

Further examples of texts which students can study to understand the position of women in the past and examine the extent to which women's roles have been determined by such writings are provided by the Bible. In Genesis (Chapter 19, vv. 1-14), Lot provides hospitality to two angels. The local men of Sodom threaten to sexually assault these two male guests. Lot intervenes and says, '(n)o, my friends, do not be so wicked. Look, I have two daughters, both virgins; let me bring them out to you, and you can do what you like with them'.

In a similar story in Judges (Chapter 19, vv. 1-30) a man says to some 'scoundrels' who want sexual intercourse with his male guests that they can have his daughter, a virgin. He says, '(r)ape her and do to her what you please; but you shall not commit such an outrage against a man.' However, instead of giving these men his daughter, the Levite guest thrusts his concubine out the door. 'They assaulted her and abused her all night till the morning, and when the dawn broke, they let her go. The girl came at daybreak and fell down at the entrance of the man's house where her master was.' She was so badly assaulted that she did not move. When the man found her he picked up a knife and cut her up into 12 pieces.

In Esther (vv. 10-22), Queen Vashti loses her position as queen because she refuses to comply with her drunken husband's demand for attendance. The King thinks his wife is beautiful and wants to show her to his courtiers. As a result of her disobedience '(l)etters were sent to all the royal provinces, to every province in its own script and to every people in their own language, in order that each man might be master in his own house and control all his own womenfolk'.

Improvisations which deal with issues of equality, gender-role stereotypes and discrimination could be used in drama lessons. One such group improvisation, as a guide to students' awareness of gender-stereotyping, might be to ask them to get into groups of four, two boys and two girls. (This exercise could be adapted to most age groups). Give each group a piece of paper which describes the four characters. It could read something like this:

Improvisation
It is 7 o'clock one November evening in the Clark family.
Character One (adult); prepares the evening meal, talks about the day he/she had, talks about the evening class she/he attends how much she/he enjoys it. He/she is a little worried by the exams in 18 months time, but this qualification will give her/him the necessary qualifications for promotion.
Character Two (student) talks about his/her A-levels due to be taken that summer, discusses which university he/she will try to get into and the degree she/he will study.
Character Three (student) tells everyone that she/he is not happy at school. He/she does not like the teacher at all and always seems to be in the teacher's bad books.
He/she says that her/his bicycle is broken and that he/she needs a new one.
Character Four (adult); arrives late, apologises, talks about her/his day and tells the gathered group that he/she has been offered a better job, more money and guaranteed promotion in 18 month's time. The job is 300 miles away.
The decision as to whether to accept the offer or not must be decided tonight.
Each take a character and work out a solution to the problem.

Planning for introducing sexual harassment into the curriculum has to be done in the same way as other topics within the schemes of work and programmes of study. Whilst each teacher has their own method of planning, I shall briefly describe one method[15] which I found especially helpful when I was a teacher. This pattern can be adapted to teaching any topic which is based on negotiating the curriculum with the learners. Many readers will be aware of the model I describe, which can be used in all subject areas and at all levels from early childhood education to planning an inservice course for staff members. The programme design gives learners the chance to negotiate aspects of the programme with the teacher. If students take part in the design process they are more likely to have a stake in the learning and feel responsible and proud of the products. Students are unlikely to want to change their attitudes and values about sexual harassment from a teacher who tells them 'this will be'. Sexual harassment awareness-raising can only be successfully undertaken when the students themselves feel that it is an important issue.

Curriculum Planning and Programming

I use seven headings when designing a programme. They are:

1 Content: What are we going to learn about?

2 Justification of the content: Why is this important?

3 Products: What do I and the students want as products at the end?

4 Skills to be built up or practised

5 Learning activities: How am I going to start this process?

6 Aids and resources: What aids and resources are available?

7 Evaluation: How are we to evaluate the process and the products?

1. Content

This is the subject to be explored, the area or territory we want the students to tackle. In this case we are planning a unit to do with sexual harassment or an allied topic area. Therefore we may choose a topic which is broader than sexual harassment *per se* and which takes into account other aspects of the phenomenon. We may choose a topic entitled 'The Position of Women in Society', 'Bullying', 'Sexism', 'Discrimination', 'Women in Literature', 'Fairy Stories', 'The Family', or 'Friends and Friendship'. The focus of such a unit will be determined by the needs of the National Curriculum, the time of year, the lessons and time available and age of the children and whether this topic will be fitting into another curriculum area such as History or English, or whether it is part of the Personal and Social Education programme.

2. Justification of the content

We must be able to be justify any topic we want the students to study in terms of its relevance and suitability. With a programme which incorporates sexual harassment there may be the need to justify the topic for not only the headteacher or the head of department, but also for parents. Of course it is extremely important that the students know why it is that they are studying such an issue, so that they are aware of its importance and relevance too. Justifying an issue such as this will lead us into contemplating what the aims of such a programme are. Why is it we want the children to study this issue and what is its relevance now? What has brought us to the conclusion that this is important? What do they already know about the subject? What new perspectives do we want to introduce?

3. Products

Some possible products which could be negotiated between us, the teacher, and the students could be: a written assignment to which the whole class contributes called 'What to do about bullying in our school'; a drama production called 'Only a Girl' which looks at discriminatory practices towards girls and women from birth to death; a class newspaper which reports on sexist and non-sexist behaviour around the school; a non-sexist pantomime; or a book of non-sexist stories for a local primary school. One group of senior students wrote a sexual harassment policy for their sixth form common room. The outcomes may, of course, be more intangible than this as you aim for a better school spirit or ethos based on mutual respect between all school personnel.

4. Skills to be built up or practised

What skills will the students be practising as they work towards the negotiated products? They could be both general and specific skills. For example, if the children do not know how to work in small groups it may be necessary to teach listening skills, recording skills or time-sharing skills. General skills which may be practised through the topic may be writing skills of planning, composing and editing. Specific skills may include how to be more assertive, how to critically appraise a book, how to develop a non-sexist eye, how to read non-verbal signs or how to communicate without using sexist language. During the process of completing the products you may find that there are unforeseen skills which need to be practised and learned, for the students may take divergent paths and in the process find that they need new skills not previously envisaged. What is important is that the skills are learned in context, rather than as skills to be practised *per se*.

5. Learning activities

The learning activities can only be decided after negotiation with the students and are contingent on their interests and commitment. By taking time to plan with them how they want to deal with the topic that you have chosen, you will provide them with the opportunity to have a stake in the learning activities and the products. Thus whilst the product may not be totally negotiable, in that they will all be doing some written work, what could be negotiated is the subject matter they write and the way in which it is presented. Similarly you may want the class to write and produce a play around the theme 'Sexism in Society', but the actual content, the improvisations and the production could all be in their hands.

6. Aids and resources

As well as using the major resources of the students' and your own experiences, information and stimulus can be obtained from:

- people in the school community such as parents, nurses, doctors, Rape Crisis Centre workers, social workers and librarians

- stories, pictures, poetry and music

- television programmes, theatre, films and videos, Drama-in-Education productions

- excursions.

7. Methods of evaluation

When negotiating the topic and how it will be approached and completed, it is important to discuss with the students the methods by which the process and the products will be evaluated. If students are involved in the evaluation they will be interested in the criteria by which judgements are made. If they know what it is you will be evaluating, for example the contents of the drama production, or the quality and level of awareness in a debate, the students will be able to work towards these ends and not be in the dark as to what it is being evaluated. An important aspect is the process by which the students arrived at the product(s). How well did they research the topic, what improvements did they make in their interviewing techniques, how much better did the groups work together at the end than at the beginning of the project?

Of course there may well be the possibility that an outside evaluator be used, such as in the case of a performance, in which an audience may be asked to respond critically to the play.

Some other methods of evaluation might be:

- keeping a journal

- small group discussions

- large group reflection

- formal testing

- asking other students from another year level to evaluate the product.

How to get started

At the outset it might look as though it would be far easier to get girls involved in a learning project about sexual harassment than it is, because it could be assumed that after seeing a few statistics or reading relevant passages they would immediately identify with the oppression and long-term detriment that sexual harassment brings[16]. However, in my experience, this is not always the case. In particular, girls of fourteen are so well established and conditioned to behave and act and think about themselves in a particular way that it is extremely difficult to effect change at a fundamental level. Of course girls of this age are vulnerable to peer-group pressure too. They may have started 'going out' with boys, be concerned with their image and will not necessarily see that they have been conditioned to behave in certain ways. With girls in primary schools this may not be so much of a problem, but for adolescent girls, as with adolescent boys, the wish to conform to their gender stereotypes is particularly strong. They have had over a decade of seeing how to be female, how to play the girl's role, how to act in a feminine way, and how to be sexually attractive to boys and young men. For this they have received positive feedback, and for you to provide them with information which is at odds with their image of themselves often produces a tirade of angry denial and further entrenchment in the female stereotype.

With boys there is a different challenge, but often a similar outcome. Even young boys have acquired the masculine habits and male attributes which have helped shape their behaviour since they were babies. They might find it hard to see any point in their changing. They are in a position of power, so why should they give up their advantage?

Getting started on any new topic, whether it be in social studies or English literature, is the same. How do we get the students committed to wanting to find out about whatever it is that the curriculum dictates? Whilst I have suggested that sexual harassment could be a topic in itself, there is still the problem of getting started. Of course there are many methods. In a situation where students themselves do not find it difficult to talk about aspects of discrimination, sexism or sexual harassment, their interest could be shaped into a scheme of work and programme of study. Maybe some of the boxes in the first three chapters could provide the starting point. Give the students, for example, the box (p. 7) which gives the statistics of the number of women secretaries, teachers, shop assistants etc. Ask them to talk about why there is such a clear distinction between jobs for men and women. What are the implications of this in terms of wages, security, promotion, pensions etc? This could well be the springboard that the students need to get involved.

References

[1] See Valerie Walkerdine and the Girls and Mathematics Unit, (1989) *Counting Girls Out*, London: Virago Press.
Leone Burton, (1986) *Girls into Maths Can Go*, London: Holt, Rinehart and Winston.
Sarah Sharkey, (1983) 'Mathematics', in Janie Whyld (ed.) *Sexism in the Secondary Curriculum*, Cambridge: Harper and Row.

[2] See Judy Samuel, (1983) 'Mathematics and Science - Introduction', in Janie Whyld (ed.) *Sexism in the Secondary Curriculum*, Cambridge: Harper and Row.

[3] See John Siraj-Blatchford and Jeremy Loud, (1990) 'A Joint Primary/Secondary Integrated Science Scheme', in Eva Tutchell (ed.) *Dolls and Dungarees*, Milton Keynes: Open University Press.

[4] See Martin Grant, (1983) 'Craft, Design and Technology', in Janie Whyld (ed.) *Sexism in the Secondary Curriculum*, Cambridge: Harper and Row.

[5] See Barbara Wynn, (1983) 'Home Economics', in Janie Whyld (ed.) *Sexism in the Secondary Curriculum*, Cambridge: Harper and Row.

6 See Breke Larsen, (1983) 'Geography', in Janie Whyld (ed.) *Sexism in the Secondary Curriculum,* Cambridge: Harper and Row.

7 See C., McLaughlin, C., Lodge and C., Watkins (1991 forthcoming), *Gender and Pastoral Care: the personal/social aspects of the whole school,* Oxford: Basil Blackwell.

8 See Christina Shamaris, (1990) 'Deepa's Story: Writing non-sexist stories for a Reception Class', in Eva Tutchell (ed.) *Dolls and Dungarees,* Milton Keynes: Open University Press.

9 Helen Vick, (1990) 'The Use of Drama in an Anti-Sexist Classroom', in Eva Tutchell (ed.) *Dolls and Dungarees,* Milton Keynes: Open University Press.

10 See Angela Holdsworth, (1988) *Out of the Dolls House: The Story of Women in the Twentieth Century,* London: BBC Books.

11 See G., Braybon and P., Summerfield (1987) *Out of the Cage: Women's Experiences in Two World Wars,* London: Pandora.
K., Charlesworth and M., Cameron (1986) *All That: The Other Half of History,* London: Pandora.
R., Miles (1990) *The Women's History of the World,* London: Paladin Grafton Books.

12 See C., Davidson (1982) *A Woman's Work is Never Done: A history of housework in the British Isles 1650-1950,* London: Chatto and Windus.

13 See J., Lewis (1984) *Women in England 1870-1950: Sexual Divisions and Social Change,* Sussex: Wheatsheaf.

14 See J., Lewis (1981) 'Women, Lost and Found: The Impact of Feminism on History', in Dale Spender (ed.) *Men's Studies Modified,* The Athene Series, Oxford: Pergamon Press.

15 Adapted from *Images of Life, a handbook about drama in education R-12.* R-12 Drama Curriculum Committee, Education Department of South Australia, 31 Flinders St., Adelaide, South Australia, 5000.

16 See L., Smith (1990) *Equality: Understanding Feminism,* London: William Collins.

CHAPTER 6

Personal Strategies

Introduction

The two previous chapters have discussed ways of tackling sexual harassment from an institutional point of view. Whilst this is important, sexual harassment also happens on a one-to-one basis and sometimes it will be necessary for individuals to take action into their own hands.

This chapter looks at some practical ways of dealing with a person or persons who perpetrate sexual harassment. Not only will there be some of the strategies I have used on sexual harassers myself, but there will also be details or some idea of how other people have acted. Although, of course, the methods of treating sexual harassers cannot be categorised into method A, B etc., there is a range of different ways of thinking about action. One of the main attributes of sexual harassment is that it is an extremely personal situation to be in, and finding a way out of it is often not easy. This chapter will provide some strategies for thinking about the options available, and then acting.

Dealing with sexual harassment

There are basically three major ways of dealing with incidents of sexual harassment: informally, formally or silently. Which one you should choose is dependent on a number of variables; the relationship of the perpetrator to you; the circumstances in which it occurs; your feelings; the actual nature of the harassment; and the likely outcomes. A further factor concerns the institution in which you study or work, and whether it has the necessary machinery to cope with a complaint.

Informal complaints

Informal complaints are those which you deal with yourself or ask a friend to deal with, but which are not lodged formally with someone who will have to deal with them as part of her or his job. Whether you feel you can deal with the harasser on your own or you need help will be dependent on whether he is a teacher or a student and your position *vis-à-vis* him. In some cases an informal approach is the best, because many men are unaware of how intrusive or patronising their behaviour has been and it only takes a person to point out the inappropriateness of this for them to stop.

Gender-role stereotyping has influenced how men believe they should behave and many have learned that it is their duty to take care of women and girls because of the myth that women and girls need looking after. Hence traditional patterns of behaviour for men and women have developed. Three simple examples of this are the opening of doors, walking on the outside of the pavement and ushering women into a room first. These are all traces of men's and women's learned socialisation and have been regarded for many years as 'good manners'. Whilst some of these traditional behaviours are gradually being eroded, and women too open doors and wait for men to go into rooms first, the beliefs about men and women's roles in society are still deeply entrenched. One of the most obvious forms of male patronage is the use of terms like 'dear', 'love' and 'petal'. To many men these are not patronising or anything to get upset about, for their intentions are honourable and they mean to make women feel comfortable. Therefore to challenge this mode of speaking is often taken by the man to be churlish and rude.

Before challenges to sexual harassers are made it is important, therefore, that you are aware of the possible ramifications. As I have said, some men and boys are keen to know how their behaviour offends and take seriously what you say to them. Others may not be so understanding and may well become extremely angry, verbally abusive or even violent, or use their rank to apply further detriment at a later stage.

I once received a postcard of a particularly unpleasant nature from a lecturer in the University at which I was a student. This arrived immediately before an exam I was about to have, of which he was to be the major examiner. I wrestled with the issue of confronting him before the examination and risking failing, or of waiting until afterwards, when, if I had failed, he may have seen my challenge as one of 'sour grapes'.

I decided on the former strategy and went to see him. He was busy and offered to come to my study as soon as he was free. When he arrived and I told him that I had found the postcard unacceptable, embarrassing, intimidating and sexually suggestive, he became extremely angry, abusive, insulting and loud. At one point I was scared that he would act violently. In this situation I had not assessed the situation accurately. Confrontations in a private space, such as a study or office, are not particularly safe as you may not be able to judge how the person will react.

Formal complaints

Formal complaints are those that are lodged with someone who is a representative of the sexual harassment policy in your institution. In most policy documents there is a list of trained personnel to whom you can go to make a complaint. They will be in a position to help you solve the grievance, to put into action the resolution process and if necessary to implement the disciplinary actions.

Confidentiality should be maintained at all times and only those directly concerned - the perpetrator, any witnesses, the recipient, and the person with whom you lodge the complaint, should know the details of the incident. Whilst these people will be entrusted to keep confidentiality, in my experience silence around such a case is extremely difficult to monitor and should not be relied upon. In a sexual harassment policy there should be a clause which discusses what action will be taken if further victimisation of the recipient occurs, or the harassment is repeated.

Doing nothing

Doing nothing is a strategy that is possible, and one you may prefer to use. That is OK. It is understandable that when women and girls receive unwanted attention from males, whose behaviour is supported by both individual and institutional power within society, they remain quiet for very good reasons. One reason for keeping quiet is because much of this kind of male behaviour is condoned and sanctioned as normal and natural, and the recipient may not identify it as sexual harassment or might believe nothing can be done about it. To make complaints is very difficult in a society where unwanted male attention is mislabelled as flattery. If a person does complain, her behaviour is often interpreted as her having no sense of humour, being priggish or a man-hater and as a consequence she may be ostracised from her social set.

If the harassment is of a jokey nature, such as is found in many schools when boys tell jokes about parts of a woman's body, or try and remove girls' jeans as a laugh, or make funny comments about periods, many young women find it difficult to separate the negative feelings of embarrassment from the positive feelings of belonging to a group. For this reason they remain quiet. Some girls not only remain quiet, they seem to be going along with it at the time, joking with boys and laughing derogatorily at some aspect of femaleness. However, if you talk to the girls afterwards, many know there is a contradiction in what they feel about the behaviour and what they do about it, but believe that for the present, at least, it is better to remain silent.

Keeping quiet about sexual harassment, however, is not reserved to shy women and girls, for it happened to me recently, following a talk I gave on sexual harassment to a group of professional women and men. The organiser, a man well into his 60s whom I had met on three or four occasions, attended the seminar. He invited me to a formal lunch party a few days later, where he made a public comment about no sexual harassment being allowed during the meal because of my presence. This publicity was

D

surprising and embarrassing, and trivialised the whole issue of sexual harassment. All present at the lunch smiled and laughed. On departing, the same man kissed me goodbye on the forehead. The frustrating point was that, even after my lecture, this man had not only not understood the issues of sexual harassment, but had subsequently harassed *me*. Further, as with many situations of this kind, I had the feeling that if I complained I might well not be given more work from this organisation.

But did I remain silent for financial or career reasons only? Of course this was one reason, but I think there are others. Women and girls are not taught to be demanding. In fact, little girls are trained to be passive, to put up with discomfort and to please others, initially their fathers and brothers, then their husbands. One of the reasons that women find it hard to ask males to stop particular behaviour is that they think it might give offence. Women do not like to be assertive, especially towards men, as this behaviour is often considered rude. Consequently they are often more likely to put up with it, than confront.

Whilst remaining silent is one alternative to confrontation its ramifications should also be considered. At an individual level, unless behaviour is challenged, it is unlikely to stop and may get worse. Alternatively, it may not get worse, in fact it may stay exactly the same, but what changes is your tolerance to it. A young woman who worked in a bank told me that her boss used to call her 'Jan Darling' whenever he spoke to her. At the beginning she thought this was polite and acceptable. As she got to know him and, in particular, his attitudes and values towards women better (he thought women should stay at home and look after the children), she began to dislike this form of address. She felt unable to ask him to stop because she had accepted it for all those months previously. Her level of distress over her boss's attitude to her and other women, symbolised in the use of the words 'Jan Darling', finally forced her into applying for another job and leaving that branch.

At a more universal level, remaining quiet does nothing to promote change in a general way of all men's behaviour. If all women were able to challenge all men's unwanted attentions successfully, then men's behaviour would have to change. Perhaps it is because so many of us remain silent that no systematic and constant pressure is brought to bear. At one institution, where I worked, a group of us made badges on which was written the slogan 'The Dear Hunters', as a protest against men calling us 'dear' and 'love'. Perhaps each institution should promote a week in which all recipients are encouraged to 'Speak out about Sexual Harassment'.

Single-sex groups

It is important to consider the case for single-sex groups when discussing issues of sexual harassment. Because sexual harassment is so closely linked with normal male behaviour, and as a consequence women and men view it so differently, it is of great value to have students in single-sex groups in order that they be given the space to discuss the issues which affect them personally. By discussing situations and sharing experiences it may be possible for boys to make a better and more informed decision as to how to act in the face of an accusation (see pp. 74-76), or for girls to have some choices as to how to react as a recipient of sexually harassing behaviour. Single-sex groups also give girls, in particular, the opportunity to recognise that sexual harassment is not a rare occurrence and that, whilst girls and women may look as if they are going along with the sexism, many don't like it but don't know how else to respond.

When girls are given the space to discuss their experiences of unwanted attention, they not only collect strategies of how to deal with particular situations, but also build up confidence and assertiveness as a group. For example, in dealing with an incident of verbal sexual harassment, such as being called 'a slag', especially in a classroom situation, a girl is more likely to be able to act swiftly and successfully against this if she feels the rest of the girls understand the double standards being perpetuated and will support her.

Similarly, boys need space to discuss their particular questions and issues relevant to them. In addition, important skills can be taught through single-sex groups which are difficult to teach in a mixed setting. Thus to teach boys to listen, to share air-time, to empathise with other students is necessary for their social development. Equally, girls need time to learn how to be more assertive, how to say 'no' (see pp. 69-70) and how to walk away. These skills are more easily taught and learned in all-girl or all-boy groups.

Dealing with a sexual harasser

Sexual harassers come in all shapes and sizes, old, young, short, fat, bald, Black, white, blonde, married, single, divorced and separated, and occupy a variety of positions. Harassers can include the headteacher or the caretaker who calls the female staff 'dear' or 'love' as well as the young boys who put a condom on a woman teacher's desk (see p. 13). There is also no pattern in what type of woman is harassed. Sexual harassment affects many women in many different situations, irrespective of the clothes they wear, their actions, behaviour, looks or age. Dealing with a man who sexually harasses you is particularly difficult when there is the necessity of retaining a professional relationship with him and when he is in a position of power. Thus, the male headteacher who calls the female staff 'ladies' and treats them in a patronising way is often more difficult to confront than the teaching colleague who tells sexist jokes. Often one of the problems with confronting someone like a male headteacher is that the behaviour has been going on for some time, even years. Like the bank worker, one teacher with whom I spoke said that on the first occasion the head had said to her, 'Can I help you, dear?' As she had been new she had felt unable to say anything for that reason. Now three years later she felt unable to say anything because she had remained silent for so long. In many cases your remaining silent is, in the perpetrator's view, tantamount to condoning his behaviour.

For teachers in schools it is recommended that sexual harassment between students, like racial harassment, not be allowed to pass unnoticed. Again, whilst a proactive policy should be adopted to stop it before it starts, in many cases you will need to be reactive, dealing with it when you see or hear it. Whilst punitive treatment is one option that we have at our disposal, it must be realised that the boys' use of sexual harassment is to do with their upbringing, social conditioning and the role modelling of others from whom they have learned it. Thus education in the form of consciousness-raising groups, individual counselling or curriculum initiatives on sexual harassment within each class or tutor group are more effective ways of changing behaviour than punitive treatment.

The relationship of the perpetrator to you

The first thing to consider when deciding what to do about a particular harasser is the relationship of the harasser to you and whether or not you are physically safe. Clearly, as a recipient of sexual harassment, you will feel differently with regard to the same treatment if the perpetrator is your boss, a teacher, an employer whilst you are on work experience, a colleague, a student or a stranger on a train going to school. However, remember, whatever the relationship of the person to you, if you feel the behaviour is embarrassing, intimidating, humiliating or unwanted and the person initiating it is in a position of power over you, then it constitutes sexual harassment.

How you deal with a person who sexually harasses you, either then or at a later time, depends on considerations of your safety and the series of alternatives that are available to you.

Confronting incidents of sexual harassment in situations where you may have something to lose is difficult, but can be effected, subtly, if necessary. Thus, when challenging behaviour, it is important that you say what you feel and why you do not like it, rather than attacking the man or his behaviour directly. Thus, 'I feel embarrassed when you kiss me', or, 'I feel irritated when you call me "love"', are two ways to tell him what you feel about his behaviour. Of course there is no certainty that he will react with equilibrium, or that this will be effective, but it may be worth a try.

Individual responses

Once you have named the behaviour as sexual harassment, one of the most useful things to do is to talk it over with a sympathetic colleague, a friend, your mother or someone who will support you and believe you.

If the harassment is being perpetrated by a teacher it may be advisable to seek teacher or parent help in lodging a complaint. If the harasser is a boy or group of boys in your class, it may be more appropriate to deal with it yourself or enlist the help of some girlfriends (see section on *Collective Responses*, p.70).

If you feel that you are not going to be believed for some reason and the harassment continues, begin to keep a diary about the behaviour, noting down the time it happened, location, any witnesses, what he did/said, what you did/said and what others did/said. When you make a complaint take this with you and show it to the person taking complaints.

At an individual level there are many strategies to use in response to a sexual harasser. These may range from requests for the behaviour to stop at a polite, but firm level, to sarcasm, swearing or shouting.

Ways to confront a sexual harasser

When confronting the harasser, the recipient should remember these points:

- Use direct eye contact.

- Speak clearly and slowly.

- State clearly the behaviour or comments which make you uncomfortable or angry and when they occurred.

- Concentrate on what you felt about the inappropriate behaviour, not on what he thought was intended.

- Do not undermine your complaint by smiling or apologising.

- Do not be concerned about damaging the perpetrator's feelings or ego.

- Do not be put off by his attempt to dismiss, trivialise or belittle your experience.

- Remember you are not a passive helpless victim: you have the right to put your views.

- Remember you did not ask for it and you did not deserve it.

- Be clear about what you want to happen now (i.e. that the behaviour should stop, confidentiality be respected and that positive working relations resume).

- Once you have finished, turn and walk away. Do not engage in an argument about what he thought he was doing, or what he thinks of you and people like you.

- If these strategies do not work, use them on the same harasser at another time and place, perhaps in the company of a friend or supporter.

If confronting the harasser person-to-person is not for you, alternative strategies might be to write a note or a letter, send him an article on sexual harassment, 'phone him up and tell him his behaviour is unwanted, or bring up the topic during a conversation when others are about.

I know of a woman who was in a cinema, and on finding a set of male fingers wandering up and down her leg, gripped them firmly, stood up and yelled; 'Does anyone own this hand? I found it on my thigh!'

Possible retorts to a sexual harasser

- 'Please do not put your arm around me, I don't like it'.

- 'Don't pinch my bottom! Is that how you usually behave?'

- 'Hands off!'

- 'I'm sorry I didn't hear you. What did you say?'

- 'Have you ever considered that that was a sexist remark?'

- 'I know you can't possibly mean that!'

Collective responses

One of the common traits of sexual harassers is that they direct their behaviour to many women, not just one. Because of this, it is clear that sexual harassment is not always a manifestation of sexual interest in a particular woman. Men or boys who sexually harass women and girls are not selective as to who is the recipient of their unwanted attentions. It has been found that often it is the same man in the office or school who is responsible for harassment of several employees or students. Because of the difficulty of identifying sexual harassment, because harassers usually harass secretively or when no one else is about, and because of society's response to sexual harassment, the recipient remains quiet about her feelings, thinking that she is the only one to be attracting this attention or that others don't seem to be minding his attentions, little knowing that the harassment is widespread and unwanted.

It is important, then, to share incidents of sexual harassment with other girls or women in the institution in which the harassment occurs. Name names, point out the harasser, tell others and generally make it clear that you know what he is doing and so do others, and that his actions will no longer be tolerated. The chances are that if he is sexually harassing you he is also sexually harassing a number of other women and girls too.

Of course there may well be a problem here. If you talk to other women or girls who are not aware of the problem of sexual harassment and who have never thought about it as unwanted, embarrassing or intimidating, then their response may well be one of disbelief or laughter at your concern over what to them is a trivial incident. Although this is difficult, there are two strategies that might help. Try to choose a person whom you think is aware. She may be a teacher who is known for her feminist views or an older student who has a name for being assertive and outspoken about women's issues. There may be an all-girls group in the school or a group of teachers working on issues of equal opportunities who could help. Alternatively you could try to explain to a friend what it is that is happening and what you feel, discussing the wider social implications of male dominance and female oppression and in this way try to raise her awareness at the same time.

Recently I was speaking to a woman about the work I did on sexual harassment and she told me that she went along with it, but only a certain way. 'After all', she said, 'people who object to wolf-whistles are really quite priggish. It doesn't do any harm does it?' In my opinion, wolf-whistles are harmful: they are intimidating, embarrassing, an invasion of one's space, an interruption and an insult. In effect, the man (or men) are letting you know that they think you are attractive. But do you want to know what strange men think about your body or your looks? What do they know about you? Do they know what you are like? Do they like your personality, your thoughts, your ideas and your sense of humour? Clearly not because they don't know you. In effect a wolf-whistle is an appraisal: they are giving your body, or parts of it, a mark out of ten and letting you know that in their eyes they think you are attractive, sexy, or just worth annoying. In other words you are being treated as a sex object.

One strategy used by a group of secretaries working in a large government office to combat the unwanted attentions of a sexual harasser, was to make his name public, but anonymously. In a casual conversation a number of the women employees found that one of their senior managers, a 55 year old man, was harassing them all in a variety of ways. He made comments about their appearances such as 'I do like it when you wear leather'. 'That little number you were wearing yesterday was really pretty'. He made sexual innuendoes too. One of the secretaries described an incident when she went into his office to confirm an appointment. She said to him, 'Mr Western, Mrs Smith has rung and confirmed the appointment for tomorrow. She is coming at 12 o'clock, is that OK?' Mr Western, with a leering grin on his face replied, 'I don't mind what time Mrs Smith comes, I just like it when they come'. Further behaviour from Mr Western included unwanted touching, stroking, patting and sexist and sexual jokes. After sharing many of their experiences with each other the secretaries decided to act collectively. After work one night they went into the men's loos and wrote with their lipstick on the mirror, 'John Western sexually harasses secretaries'. In the morning there was apparently a stunned silence from the men as each made a visit to the lavatory and found the accusation. John Western modified his behaviour.

The discussion of incidents of sexual harassment among women or girls in the same work institution or school allows for collective strength to build. If a woman or girl knows that she is not alone, that this treatment is not unique to her and the harassment is generally, not specifically, directed, she is likely to become more confident about dealing with it, either alone or with others. In a group of women, strategies can be brain-stormed and the most appropriate one selected to put into practice, taking account of the particular harasser, his *modus operandi* and the institution in which it is occurring.

Union representation

One possible strategy to use, if you are a recipient of sexual harassment, is to contact your union. Teachers' unions take the matter of sexual harassment seriously. They have policies which make explicit their views on sexual harassment and which give advice on what to do. The NUT, for example, has a Union's Code of Professional Conduct which states that it is unprofessional 'for any teacher to harass sexually another teacher or pupil'.

Whilst informal proceedings are recommended so that a complaint can be resolved quickly, this is not always possible and formal proceedings are then needed. At this stage it will be necessary to contact your school representative, the local negotiating secretary, an officer of your local association, the Executive member for your area or your Regional Official. They will be able to give you appropriate advice and support on what action to take. The action may include the use of the LEA's or governing body's grievance procedure.

The legal position

Sexual harassment in Britain can be unlawful in some cases. The policy statement written by the National Association of Schoolmasters and Women Teachers, (NASUWT) states:

> 'Under employment legislation, persistent sexual harassment, resulting in intolerable working conditions, is conduct which might entitle a victim to resign and claim constructive dismissal. A claim can also be, made under the Sex Discrimination Act. For sexual harassment to be unlawful discrimination (and therefore, actionable), the complainant has to be able to show that, as a direct result of the harassment, or by the reaction to it, she/he has suffered a tangible job detriment, dismissal, forced resignation, lost promotion prospects, denial of other employment benefits, etc.' NASUWT (1990).

© Angela Martin, reproduced by permission of Leeds Postcards: Leeds

A case of sexual harassment, assault or incest?

The difference between sexual assault, sexual harassment and incest is not merely a question of degree, i.e. that one is worse than the others. Whilst sexual harassment includes behaviour such as unwanted touching it can, in some cases, be identical to sexual assault or incest. The main difference between sexual harassment and the other two is that harassment is often regarded as work-based (although this is a particularly restrictive definition), usually involving a man in a position of power who is known to the recipient. Definitions of sexual assault are not limited to specific locations, although between married couples in their home sexual assault (domestic violence) is hard to prove, given the current legal system. Incest, however, is usually taken to mean any unlawful sexual activity between an adult and a younger relative when the adult is in a position of trust. (Victims of incest can also be those who, for physical or mental reasons, are not in a position to make a rational decision for themselves).

I was recently involved in an unpleasant incident involving unwanted sexual attention which could have been described variously as sexual assault or sexual harassment. I was on a train in France when a man came and sat next to me. During the course of the journey and whilst I was reading, his hand appeared under my left arm and fondled my breast. His movements were stealthy, secretive and so slow that I couldn't be sure that he was actually touching me until I looked down. He had a lecherous look on his face. I leapt up, brushing his hand from me and shouted. He ran away, but I was not prepared to leave it there. Whilst I could have called the gendarmes, and this option was offered, I chose to ask the train's guard to admonish him. With the help of an interpreter, the guard and myself confronted the harasser, and although he denied it, he looked extremely embarrassed and humiliated. The incident shows how it is possible to do something about sexual harassment in a public place, in a way which at least gives back one's autonomy and confidence. Whether or not these actions would stop the harasser from attempting a similar attack on another woman is only speculation, but I have a hunch he found the confrontation particularly embarrassing.

If for reasons of clarity, we take this example of unwanted attention, *a man'' hand on a woman's breast,* there can be a number of different interpretations applied, depending on the recipient's age, the age of the perpetrator and the relationship of the perpetrator to the recipient, although where one offence begins and another ends is difficult to judge and is usually context-bound.

Let us look at the different interpretations of this particular unwanted behaviour. Whilst in my case the man's behaviour could have been defined as sexual assault, and I could have pressed charges, to have pursued that line would have meant involving the police, gathering witnesses, statements and consequent delay. As I had no witnesses, I was on holiday, I did not speak French and I did not consider the matter to be very serious, I chose to take the action into my own hands.

However it must be remembered that sexual assault is a criminal offence and can affect men and women alike. A charge of sexual assault could, for example, be pressed on a man who puts his arms around a young woman walking across a park and kisses her. A similar charge could be made against a woman doing the same thing to a man.

If, however, the perpetrator was a male teacher and the recipient a female student, this behaviour would be sexual abuse and could be dealt with through the social services or the police. Because the teacher is in a position of responsibility and is *in loco parentis,* it is especially serious, for he is abusing his position as an adult, a teacher and a guardian.

If both the recipient and the perpetrator were students and the behaviour came to the attention of the school management, it would most probably be dealt with as sexual harassment, and whilst the female student could press charges, the likelihood is that this would not be recommended because of the lack of witnesses, the age of the perpetrator, prolonging the case and detrimental effect on the recipient.

If, however, the perpetrator of the unwanted sexual attention was a relative such as a father, stepfather, grandfather or brother and the recipient was a girl under the age of 16, then behaviour of this kind would constitute incest. In the event that the perpetrator was a woman (although statistically the number of women abusers is extremely low) and the recipient her son, and she fondled his genitals, then too incest would have been committed.

For boys: how not to be a sexual harasser

Sexual harassment is unwanted attention, often with a sexual component. Girls and women do not ask to be sexually harassed, they do not provoke it and they do not wear particular clothes because they want to be wolf-whistled. They may ask for sexual attention from people they like or want to get to know, but this is a very different matter from sexual harassment. A similar situation would be to compare a friendly rough and tumble with some friends to being beaten up by a group of thugs, when you had no power, no way out and it hurt.

When girls and young women want sexual attention they, like you, show it. They do this in a variety of ways, from the clothes they wear, to the way they toss their hair and the looks they give. These are called 'non-verbal' cues and you are probably aware of giving non-verbal cues too. Non-verbal cues are often subtle and sometimes difficult to understand. If you do confuse non-verbal cues and get accused of sexual harassment, the first thing to do is apologise sincerely and quickly. Sexual harassment is unwanted and involves the use of power to control another person. Girls and women do not ask to be pinched, kissed, touched, propositioned or have jokes made about their bodies by boys or men they do not know or like. Try to imagine a situation in which a girl was interested in you and constantly touched you, made sexual comments about your body and persistently asked you out. You do not like her and do not want to go out with her. If you asked her to stop touching you and told her that you did not want to go out with her, you would expect the behaviour to stop. This is exactly the same situation for her. Next time you ask a girl or young woman to go out with you, listen to the words she says and watch the non-verbal signs she is giving you. If she says 'no' she means 'no'. She does not mean 'I am playing hard to get'.

It is interesting that stories, myths and even songs have been made up about women who say 'no'. There is one song called '*O No John*' which is about a young woman (described as a *creature*), whose initial 'no' to an invitation goes unheeded. The song implies that the woman wanted to say 'yes' all the time, and that the man was really clever with the manipulation of words to get her to be his wife (see Appendix 2).

What is sexual harassment for one person is not necessarily so for another. This is logical, if you think about it. With someone you care about and who cares for you, touching, patting, kissing and intimate comments are an important and necessary part of your relationship. These behaviours might not be appropriate with someone else. Sexual relationships are reciprocal. Sexual harassment is a one-way operation; from the harasser to the harassed.

Similarly, you may have some close friends who are girls, at school, whom you hug, touch, to whom you give compliments, and to whom you tell 'dirty' jokes. You and they have a reciprocal relationship. They know you and like you. They trust you. Behaving with them in a close way does not constitute sexual harassment.

If one of your female classmates is being touched or patted by a friend, this does not mean that she wants you to do the same thing. Everyone is different and everyone has a different relationship with everybody else. The relationship that they have together is theirs. To go up to the girl and treat her in the same way could well be sexually harassing. The definition of sexual harassment lies with the person who perceives it as such, not with the person who is doing it. It has nothing to do with your intentions, or what you thought you were doing.

There are also some pertinent strategies for not sexually harassing strangers, or other women and girls in the street, pubs or discos:

> • Try never to frighten a woman when she is walking in the street alone at night by walking too close behind her. You could try

crossing the road, waiting a few moments so that she can go ahead, or taking another route.

• Don't leer, or stare at women or girls for example, on buses, in the street or in pubs.

• Don't wolf-whistle, grunt or make audible comments about women or girls or about their clothes, their hair or their bodies.

• If you hear someone say 'Have you heard the one about ...?', say, 'I don't want to hear it if it is sexist or racist'.

• If you are unsure of how a woman or girl finds your behaviour, try asking.

• If you ask a woman out, or to have a drink, and she says 'no', leave it at that, don't pester her.

• Don't sit or stand too close to women and girls on public transport.

Conclusion

Well, I hope the book has been useful. I have tried to put in as much helpful material as possible, whilst getting the right balance between why sexual harassment happens and what you can do about it. It is extremely important to understand the nature of institutional power and individual power which, when combined, provide the environment for harassment to occur and that in order to eliminate this behaviour it has to be approached at both levels consistently.

I am conscious that a few people may have been alienated, especially men, who find it difficult to identify with the image of the male perpetrator in this book. I wish to address this problem now. One of my personal beliefs is that one has to have militant outriders to make marginal gains. This book has tried to take a militant approach and, in the process, has not been particularly kind to or understanding of men and men's individual concerns. Rather it has lumped them all together and taken an undifferentiated, hard-hitting approach in dealing with sexual harassment.

But I have worked with men, a few, who are extremely concerned about the predicament of men and boys within the scheme of things. Some I have spoken to are embarrassed by their own sex, incredulous that some can behave in such insensitive ways. In my opinion these are the men of the future and it is those with whom I have worked and talked that I thank for being brave in the face of so much public pressure to conform to the patriarchal stereotype. It cannot be easy living out there on a limb, and as strong and assertive women who want change know, scorn from one's own sex often hurts the most.

But it is important to remember that, for women, sexual harassment is a crippling disability. If women were not controlled socially, financially, educationally and politically because of sexual harassment, school staffrooms, corridors and classrooms would be very different places. Because sexual harassment is often unpredictable in its form, frequency and location women can never be sure when, why or how it will happen. As a consequence they are often unsure in their communications with men or boys, they are unsure when it is safe or expedient to rebuff unwanted gestures, comments or looks and therefore often spend time worrying about their vulnerability. Under these conditions they can hardly fulfil their potential in various aspects of their lives. When we demand and get equal opportunities society will be fundamentally different.

A school of the future

Casting one's mind into the future and imagining a sexual-harassment-free school is both fanciful and hypothetical, for as has been already discussed, schools are microcosms of society and therefore do not exist in isolation. So to hypothesise about a school such as this can only be in a dream world, but none-the-less a dream worth a moment or two of thought. So what would a school look like where there was no sexual harassment?

First, staff and students would understand the causes and effects of sexual harassment and would be careful about their own behaviour. They would be sensitive about the impact of their behaviour on others and take care when meeting new people. There would be no sarcastic comments, putdowns, teasing, bullying, sexist remarks, jokes or innuendoes. People would have a respect for themselves and their own behaviour as well as for each other.

Second, as new people arrived in the school there would be an immediate and accessible training programme for them about the school's policy and grievance procedure. This would be available for all school personnel, staff, students, parents and governors. All levels of people, including young students, would be involved in the training process.

Third, there would be an accepted code of conduct agreed upon by school personnel which would apply to all areas of the school: the staffroom, the corridors, classrooms and the playground. This would be reviewed frequently, at least annually.

Fourth, the school administration would strive to avoid running the school in an hierarchical, patronising or male-dominated way. Many more women would be in senior positions and there would be a commitment to democratic principles of management, negotiation and conciliation.

Fifth, all staff and students would be able to recognise sexually-harassing behaviour if they came across it and, if they could not deal with it themselves, would know where to go for help.

Sixth, all personnel would know how to handle grievances made about them, and to change their behaviour accordingly.

Seventh, sexual harassment, sexual discrimination and sexism would be addressed directly and as part of the planned curriculum, at all year levels. Students and staff would be able to discuss the issues in a non-threatening environment and in a way which examined the historical, social and cultural contexts in which sexual harassment occurred. The challenging of sexually harassing behaviour would be the responsibility of all personnel in the school. Teachers, in particular, would have a responsibility to talk with perpetrators and discuss their behaviour. There would be a person available at all times to deal with cases of sexual harassment in an educative, not punitive way.

Last, and in a couple of generations' time, elderly staff members would look back on the 1990s and recount their own experiences of sexual harassment at school. The current students will look aghast and say; 'Oh, I don't believe a word of what you are saying. That's a fairy story. No one would have treated women and girls like that. Men have more respect for women than to put them down in that fashion, and anyway, I can't imagine that women would have put up with it'.

APPENDIX 1

Vignettes and Myths

Introduction

This appendix is a collection of ideas and information. I have gathered together some of the examples of sexual harassment I have come across as a teacher and adviser, as well as the common myths and assumptions I am always meeting about sexual harassment. The ten vignettes, all taken from real life, illustrate the many ways in which sexual harassment occurs in schools and illustrates how it can affect any female, from those who are very young, to older women teachers in schools. Further, sexual harassment crosses all class barriers and is not confined to women or girls who are pretty. Perpetrators too, come in all shapes and sizes, old and young.

Real examples of sexual harassment

> ### Tony
> The class was a year of 15-year-olds. For some time the class had been arguing; the boys against the girls. When the teacher asked what was going on there was silence from both parties. The split in the class became more prominent, but still no one talked about it.
> Eventually one of the boys, Tony, told the teacher that he was feeling frightened because a group of boys had got hold of some 'soft porn' magazines and were tormenting the girls. He pleaded with him not to tell the class because he felt he would be beaten up for 'splitting'.

Clara

Clara was late to an English class. The English teacher Mr Matthews, who was also the head, asked her why. Clara's reason for being six minutes late was that she had been to the girls' lavatory because she had her period and she was bleeding very heavily. She was reluctant to say this out loud to all her class so she didn't reply. The head teacher got angry and said that, as she had no excuse, she would have a detention. Clara refused to attend the detention because she felt that it was an unfair punishment. Two days later she was expelled.

John Williams

A good-looking, young male PE teacher, John Williams, was overheard to say to Joanne, a fourth year girl who was shouting in the corridor: 'Joanne, pretty girls shouldn't shout and scream like that, it's not very ladylike'.

When confronted by a colleague about his sexist language his reply was: 'But the strategy works. It stops her shouting, she blushes and thinks I'm flattering her. She likes it. I've given her a compliment in telling her that she is pretty, so she behaves more appropriately. By telling her off in another way she would have taken it badly and there would have been a nasty incident. This way everyone is happy. You can't tell me that you don't use flirting as a strategy for controlling students!'

Maria

Maria was a Bulgarian girl who had been at school in England for about six months. She was on an accelerated programme in order to do her GCSE and A Levels in two years. She was an intelligent student but had problems with certain aspects of colloquial English, in particular swear words.

She went on a school geography trip where one of the boys, John, asked her if he could 'fuck' her. She apparently said 'yes' at the request, because she didn't understand what he meant. The following day John ordered her to go outside and lie down in the grass. He told her to hurry up because he wanted to play football when he had finished.

She realised what he meant and refused. John told her that if she didn't he would tell all the other students at school that she had anyway, because she had verbally agreed to it and consequently she was a 'slag'.

Maria stayed away from school for five days after this incident because she did not want to be labelled a 'slag'. Apparently on John's return to school he carried out his threat and told other students that Maria had had sex with him and that because of this she was an 'easy lay' and a 'slag'.

Mr Webb
Before a lesson on soldering, Mr Webb told the class that he was going to do a demonstration involving dangerous and hot metal. They were not to disturb him. During the class some girls began giggling. He stopped and said, 'What is wrong with you girls? Are you bleeding?' When asked by the headteacher to explain his language and the innuendo he had made he said that he had meant: 'Were the girls injured?'

Cathy
Cathy, a five-year-old is chased by a group of boys every break-time at a small private school. The gang pick on one girl at a time, chase her, cut her off from her friends and lift her skirt. They then try and touch her pants. She doesn't tell her mother or her teacher because she doesn't think it would do any good.

Mr Black
Some sixth form girls doing A Level biology told their tutor that the biology teacher, when teaching them about reproduction, said, 'look, if I was to put my penis in your vagina the result may be a baby'. The tutor wanted the girls to make a formal complaint but they pleaded with him not to say anything. Because of the school policy on sexual harassment which assured students of confidentiality for recipients, he remained silent.

Ms Daniels
Ms Daniels was a probationary teacher. Her assessment for her first year lay with the head of department who was a man. Sometimes in the staffroom he used to say in a very loud voice so that everyone could hear, 'And how is the voluptuous *Miz* Daniels this morning?' Ms Daniels found his behaviour threatening, embarrassing and rude but was reluctant to make a complaint in case it had an effect on her report.

Girls
In many classrooms around Britain, boys call girls 'slags', 'tarts', 'sluts', 'dogs', 'cows' and 'bitches' for no other reason than that of intimidation.

Myths about sexual harassment

> Sexual harassment is not really an important issue. It doesn't hurt anyone.

Sexual harassment is an important social issue for three main reasons. First, sexual harassment does hurt. Women who suffer from sexual harassment experience a range of physical and psychological ailments including headaches, ulcers, other stomach problems, depression, tension and frustration. For students at school who are victims of sexual harassment the consequences may be reduced concentration during class, dropping certain subjects, dropping out of school, or reluctance to go on to further study.

Second, sexual harassment can have economic consequences for the recipient. If she leaves school or truants because of sexual harassment she may not get the necessary qualifications she needs for a secure job. As a result, she may only be able to find unskilled work or she may be passed over for promotion for lack of qualifications. A woman who is being sexually harassed may decide to hand in her notice. This could be detrimental to her career and be a waste of staff and training for the company.

Third, a consequence of known sexual harassment in an institution is that it has an effect on all the others working there too. If the environment is one in which people do not feel safe, work or study will not be at its best.

> That wasn't sexual harassment. I was only joking, and she knows I was only messing about. She likes it, anyway.

A particular behaviour can be seen in very different ways by men and women or boys and girls. If a woman/girl believes that she has been sexually harassed it is up to the school to take her complaint seriously. Just because a man/boy claims that she liked his attention is no indication that her perception is faulty. Sexual harassment is not based on intentionality.

> Sexual harassment! Don't be ridiculous! It's only natural for men to make a pass at women. You can't change human nature.

Sexual harassment has nothing to do with human nature. People are not born knowing how to sexually harass others. It is because of the male and female roles ascribed to and learned by men and women in our society that there is confusion as to what is natural male behaviour and what is learned behaviour. Sexual harassment is learned social behaviour, learned within the context of a sexist and patriarchal environment. If sexist practices and sexual discrimination were eradicated sexual harassment too would stop. Nor has sexual harassment got anything to do with sexual attraction, genuine expressions of affection or consensual flirting between people. A great many people meet their future partner in the workplace, but people do not form loving relationships with people who sexually harass them.

Sexual harassment can only be defined as such when there is actual physical contact.

There are many different behaviours which constitute sexual harassment. As it is the recipient of the behaviour who decides whether or not she feels sexually harassed, it is important to give the woman or girl the autonomy to decide. Behaviour or actions which constitute sexual harassment take many forms and can include requests for sexual favours, leers, physical contact, sexist remarks, dirty jokes, pin-ups, explicit sexual comments, innuendo and remarks about a woman's body. Verbal sexual harassment, for example, is a form of harassment frequently ignored by people in positions of power. One way of eradicating verbal harassment would be the avoidance of sexist language and sexist terms of address to women and girls. Some such terms are 'love', 'dear', 'little lady' or 'girl' when, in fact, the person is over the age of 18, or the use of the word 'lady' to describe a woman.

The girls should tell us if they don't like it. If they did we would stop.

It is hardly fair to expect the recipient of sexual harassment to take responsibility for male behaviour, especially if the boy or boys are in a position of power over her. Sexual harassment has the effect of silencing girls because they are afraid, if they complain, of being told that they provoked it, they have no sense of humour, they are exaggerating, or even worse, lying. Women are also afraid of victimisation.

That wasn't sexual harassment: I was just paying her a compliment.

Sexual harassment is in the eye of the beholder. If a woman or girl feels uncomfortable with a comment made, it is an indication that it was inappropriate. It is important to recognise the difference between behaviour which might be accepted by one woman or girl and how the same behaviour will be accepted by another. To a great extent sexual harassment is context-bound and is dependent on the relationship between the recipient and the perpetrator, as well as other variables such as status, authority, position, etc. Also it is important to recognise the difference in behaviour which might be accepted in more personal situations from that which is appropriate in the workplace.

> Look, what I was doing was only a bit of fun. It wasn't meant to be taken seriously. She should have a sense of humour.

This statement implies that sexual harassment is 'harmless fun'. It is not. It is degrading and humiliating. Sexual harassment means being treated as a sex object not as a worker/student. Some people confuse sexual harassment with flirtation. It is important to make the distinction. Flirtation can be harmless fun. But, the prerequisite is that the interest be mutual and no intimidation involved. It is not fun or funny to be subjected to unwanted behaviour. It is not 'harmless' to harass women or girls verbally, or to pinch or pat them.

> Slags can't be sexually harassed.

Research shows that sexual harassment has nothing to do with age, looks, body size, clothes, location or time. Any woman or girl can be sexually harassed. No one 'asks' to be humiliated, threatened and embarrassed. What a woman/girl wears, where she walks, the time she goes out, who she goes out with is her decision and does not give anyone licence to sexually harass.

> A person being sexually harassed can always say 'no'.

Unfortunately the recipients of sexual harassment are often not in positions to say 'no' and for their words and actions to be respected. Sexual harassment occurs between people who are not equal. Most often the harasser has economic and/or physical power over the woman. From this position he can also control the reprisals.

Further, one of the supporting myths about women is that when they say 'no' they really mean 'yes'. This myth has occurred as a result of the roles in our society. Men are often seen as the sexual predators whilst women are regarded as the prey. Thus if women say 'no' some men believe that they do not mean it but are really playing hard to get. No one has the right to impose their own needs and desires on someone who has indicated an unwillingness to accept an invitation. It is an intrusion and an invasion of their rights and privacy.

> If girls go into places where they are not welcome, like the woodwork room, then they should expect to be sexually harassed.

Girls in schools have the right to be respected wherever they go within the school. They also have the right to be provided with equal opportunities to all the school facilities. The science or computer labs, the weight-training gym and the woodwork rooms are not the sole domain of males. When girls leave school many are now seeking careers in areas which until recently were male-dominated. As we have seen, many of these jobs are better paid, more secure and provide a career structure.

> Sexual harassment! I wish I could get some.

Sexual harassment is unwanted attention. Women and girls do not like being sexually harassed. Do men or boys like being bullied? Sexual harassment is not the same as sexual attention. Many people like sexual attention and use many devices to get it. One of the devices is wearing particular clothes. However, this does not mean that the woman who is wearing attractive clothes wants sexual attention from you! Remember, sexual attention can be funny, sexy, intimate and clandestine but, above all, it is wanted. Sexual harassment is an unacceptable form of social interaction and is unwanted sexual pestering which is intimidating, frightening and humiliating.

> Sexual harassment my foot! Boys will be boys, you know!

One of the problems with sexual harassment is that it is seen to be a normal and natural way for men, and boys in particular, to behave. Boys, for example, are encouraged to 'sow their wild oats' and to be sexually experienced before they settle down for marriage. However, although many people in society would have us believe that men are naturally more sexually active than women, this myth was born in the nineteenth century when it really was thought that men would become ill if their wives did not allow them their conjugal rights and they had to suppress their sexual desires (see box p. 38, about William Acton). However, as sexual harassment has little to do with sexual pleasure, but is rather an expression of power and domination and is perpetrated often by the same man on many different women in one office or school, to claim that sexual harassment is a result of men's sexual appetite is fallacious, antiquated and incorrect.

> All the girls I know go along with it so they must be enjoying it.

Women are often silent about the experience of sexual harassment. They are unlikely to speak out to ask the person to stop, especially if that man is in a position of power over her. Women and girls also have been taught not to object to male behaviour for they have learned that this is normal and natural. Further, because of their training as females, women and girls often have different ways of expressing discomfort and embarrassment. Many girls and women smile, giggle, look down, play with their hair or fiddle with their clothes. These actions do not mean they are enjoying it. Men and boys are much more likely to speak out about things they don't like.

> Sexual harassment is very rare. I don't know anybody who has been sexually harassed.

Sexual harassment is not a rare phenomenon. What is still unusual is for sexual harassment to be properly labelled and to be taken seriously. Until people are given the opportunity to define sexual harassment and to talk about their unwanted experiences many women are likely to say they have not been a recipient of sexual harassment. Women often do not have the language or information to describe sexually harassing behaviour. However, research which has been carried out in universities, employment centres and businesses shows that sexual harassment in the workplace happens frequently.

> If you ignore sexual harassment it will go away.

Because sexual harassment is behaviour which is based on the abuse of power in order to control women, remaining silent about such behaviour does not stop it. In fact often the opposite occurs. If the woman ignores sexually harassing behaviour the perpetrator believes that his messages are not being received, so the unwanted attention gets worse or more frequent.

APPENDIX 2

Ideas

Introduction

Here is a selection of poetry and prose, some taken from classic texts, others from more modern sources, which could fit into a variety of subject areas for discussion about sexual harassment in particular, or sexual discrimination generally.

Extracts from literature

Thomas Hardy: Tess of the d'Urbervilles.

Tess (Chp 8) is one example of a woman who is sexually harassed by a man who is in a position of power over her and uses coercion and threat to get sexual favours.

'Having mounted beside her Alec d'Urberville drove rapidly along the crest of the hill, chatting compliments to Tess as they went, the cart with her box being left far behind. Rising still, an immense landscape stretched around them on every side; behind, the green valley of her birth, before a gray country of which she knew nothing except from her first brief visit to Trantridge. Thus they reached the verge of an incline down which the road stretched in a long straight descent of nearly a mile.

Ever since the accident with her father's horse Tess Durbeyfield, courageous as she naturally was, had been exceedingly timid on wheels; the least irregularity of motion startled her. She began to get uneasy at a certain recklessness in her conductor's driving.

"You will go down slow, sir, I suppose?" she said with attempted unconcern.

D'Urberville looked round upon her, nipped his cigar with the tips of his large white centre-teeth, and allowed his lips to smile slowly of themselves.

"Why, Tess", he answered, after another whiff or two, "it isn't a brave bouncing girl like you who asks that? Why, I always go down at full gallop. There's nothing like it for raising your spirits."

"But perhaps you need not now".

"Ah", he said, shaking his head,"there are two to be reckoned with. It is not me alone. Tib has to be considered, and she has a very queer temper".

"Who?"

"Why, this mare. I fancy she looked round at me in a very grim way just then. Didn't you notice it?"

"Don't try to frighten me, sir" said Tess stiffly.

"Well I don't. If any living man can manage this horse I can- I won't say any living man can do it - but if such has the power, I am he."

"Why do you have such a horse?"

"Ah, well may you ask! It was my fate, I suppose. Tib has killed one chap; and just after I bought her she nearly killed me. And then, take my word for it, I nearly killed her. But she's touchy still, very touchy; and one's life is hardly safe behind her sometimes."

They were just beginning to descend; and it was evident that the horse, whether of her own will or of his (the latter being the more likely), knew so well the reckless performance expected of her that she hardly required a hint from him.

Down, down, they sped, the wheels humming like a top, the dog-cart rocking right and left, its axis acquiring a slightly oblique set in relation to the line of progress; the figure of the horse rising and falling in undulations before them. Sometimes a wheel was off the ground, it seemed, for many yards; sometimes a stone was sent spinning over the hedge, and flinty sparks from the horse's hoofs outshone the daylight. The aspect of the straight road enlarged with their advance, the two banks dividing like a splitting stick; one rushing past at each shoulder.

The wind blew through Tess's white muslin to her very skin, and her washed hair flew out behind. She was determined to show no open fear, but she clutched d'Urberville's rein-arm.

"Don't touch my arm! We shall be thrown out if you do! Hold on round my waist!"

She grasped his waist, and so they reached the bottom.

"Safe, thank God in spite of your fooling!" said she, her face on fire.

"'Tis truth."

"Well, you need not let go your hold of me so thanklessly the moment you feel yourself out of danger".

She had not considered what she had been doing: whether he were man or woman, stick or stone, in her involuntary hold on him. Recovering her reserve she sat without replying, and thus they reached the summit of another declivity.

"Now then, again!" said d'Urberville.

"No, no!" said Tess. "Show more sense, do, please."

"But when people find themselves on one of the highest points in the county, they must get down again," he retorted.

He loosened rein, and away they went the second time. D'Urberville turned his face to her as they rocked, and said, in playful raillery: "Now then put your arms round my waist again, as you did before, my Beauty."

"Never!" said Tess independently, holding on as well as she could without touching him.

"Let me put one little kiss on those holmberry lips, Tess, or even on that warmed cheek, and I'll stop - on my honour, I will!"

Tess, surprised beyond measure, slid further back still on her seat, at which he urged the horse anew, and rocked her the more.

"Will nothing else do?" she cried at length, in desperation, her large eyes staring at him like those of a wild animal. This dressing her up so prettily by her mother had apparently been to lamentable purpose.

"Nothing, dear Tess," he replied.

"Oh, I don't know - very well: I don't mind!" she panted miserably.

He drew rein, and as they slowed he was on the point of imprinting the desired salute, when, as if yet aware of her own modesty, she dodged aside. His arms being occupied with the rein there was left him no power to prevent her manoeuvre.

"Now, damn it - I'll break both our necks!" swore her capriciously passionate companion. "So you can go from your word like that, you young witch, can you?"

"Very well", said Tess, "I'll not move since you be so determined! But I thought you would be kind to me, and protect me, as my kinsman!"

"Kinsman be hanged! Now!"

"But I don't want anybody to kiss me, sir!" she implored, a big tear beginning to roll down her face. "And I wouldn't ha' come if I had known!"

He was inexorable, and she sat still, and d'Urberville gave her the kiss of mastery. No sooner had he done so than she flushed with shame, took out her handkerchief, and wiped the spot on her cheek that had been touched by his lips. His ardour was nettled at the sight, for the act on her part had been unconsciously done.

"You are mighty sensitive for a cottage girl!" said the young man.'

William Shakespeare: Othello

Women are often portrayed as conniving, dishonest and mystically seductive. In *Othello*, Desdemona is a strong woman who is mistrusted by Othello. Evidence of her dishonesty is apparent when she disobeys her father by marrying against his wishes. Othello uses this as evidence of her deceit, and murders her. Women, as I have already mentioned (see pp. 4-5), were owned first by their fathers and second by their husbands and as such were at their mercy. Look for other female characters in Shakespeare's plays and see how they are described. For example look at Ophelia in *Hamlet*, Cleopatra in *Anthony and Cleopatra*, Cordelia, in *King Lear*, Titania in *A Midsummer Night's Dream*, Lady Macbeth in *Macbeth*, Juliet in *Romeo and Juliet*, and Katharina in *The Taming of the Shrew*.

E

(Act 1 Scene i, 169)	(Act 111 Scene iii, 206-208)
'Brabantio: O treason of the blood Fathers, from hence trust not your daughters' minds By what you see them act. Are there not charms By which the property of youth and maidenhood May be abus'd? Have you not read, Roderigo, Of some such things?'	'Iago: She did deceive her father, marrying you: And when she seem'd to shake and fear your looks, She lov'd them most.'

Charlotte Brontë: Jane Eyre

In Chapter 1, Charlotte Brontë writes about Jane's early life as an orphan and her experience. In today's terminology could this be labelled sexual harassment? She is 10, John Reed, a schoolboy of 14.

'John had not much affection for his mother and sisters, and an antipathy to me. He bullied and punished me; not two or three times in the week, not once or twice in a day, but continuously: every nerve I had feared him, and every morsel of flesh on my bones shrank when he came near. There were moments when I was bewildered by the terror he inspired, because I had no appeal whatever against his menaces or his inflictions; the servants did not like to offend their young master by taking my part against him, and Mrs Reed was blind and deaf on the subject: she never saw him strike or heard him abuse me, though he did both now and then in her very presence; more frequently behind her back' C. Brontë (1966, p. 42).

Jane also speaks out strongly about the role and place of women in society.

'It is in vain to say human beings ought to be satisfied with tranquillity: they must have action; and they will make it if they cannot find it. Millions are condemned to a stiller doom than mine, and millions are in silent revolt against their lot. Nobody knows how many rebellions besides political rebellions ferment in the masses of life which people earth. Women are supposed to be very calm generally: but women feel just as men feel; they need exercise for their faculties, and a field for their efforts as much as their brothers do; they suffer from too rigid a restraint, too absolute a stagnation, precisely as men would suffer, and it is narrow-minded in their privileged fellow-creatures to say that they ought to confine themselves to making puddings and knitting stockings, to play the piano and embroider bags. It is thoughtless to condemn them, or laugh at them, if they seek to do more or learn more than custom has produced necessary for their sex' C. Brontë (1966, p. 141).

D. H. Lawrence

D. H. Lawrence's descriptions of women are often ones which depict them as greedy, dominating and possessive. Here are two extracts. Perhaps it would be interesting to have the students compare Lawrence's perception of women's lust for the possession of flowers with men's ownership of women.

'But it seemed to him, woman was always so horrible and clutching, she had such a lust for possession, a greed of self-importance in love. She wanted to have, to own, to control, to be dominant. Everything must be referred back to her, to Woman, the Great Mother of everything, out of whom proceeded everything and to whom everything must finally be rendered up' D. H. Lawrence (1966, p224).

'The collier fled out of the house as soon as he could, away from the nagging materialism of the woman. With the women it was always: This is broken, now you've got to mend it! or else: We want this, that and the other, and where is the money coming from? The collier didn't know and didn't care very deeply - his life was otherwise. So he escaped. He roved the countryside with his dog, prowling for a rabbit, for nests, for mushrooms, anything. He loved the countryside, just the indiscriminating feel of it. Or he loved just to sit on his heels and watch - anything or nothing. He was not intellectually interested. Life for him did not consist in facts, but in a flow. Very often, he loved his garden. And very often he had a genuine love of the beauty of flowers. I have known it often and often, in colliers.

Now the love of flowers is a very misleading thing. Most women love flowers as possessions, and as trimmings. They can't look at a flower, and wonder a moment, and pass on. If they see a flower that arrests their attention, they must at once pick it, pluck it. Possession! A possession! Something added on to *me*! And most of the so-called love of flowers today is merely this reaching out of possession and egoism: something I've *got*: something that embellishes *me*. Yet I've seen many a collier stand in his back garden looking down at a flower with that odd, remote sort of contemplation which shows *real* awareness of the presence of beauty. It would not even be admiration, or joy, or delight, or any of those things which so often have a root in the possessive instinct. It would be a sort of contemplation: which shows the incipient artist' A.A.H. Inglis (ed.) (1971, pp.107-108).

Poems by women and about women

Have Faith in your Daughter[1]

One day in June last summer
I found I was the Rose Queen's mother
Of course I had said, "but looks don't count
It's kindness, character", --- but she'd found out
Ways of dealing with feminist mums.

All freckles, Celtic charm and cheek
She won, leaving me on the day, the freak
Of the show, while she, in satin gown and crown
Enjoyed the fuss as the prettiest girl in town,
And it was, in its way, a classic occasion.

Teacakes and teacups, side stalls and sun
A stern-looking vicar disapproving of fun
A local JP with friends in high places and fingers in pies
Giving out prizes, telling some lies
About his ideals. I tried to hide.

It was with relief that I realized the Rose Queen
Saw the irony too --- that my lessons hadn't been
Totally lost. She thought it wrong it took
Drawings and stories to judge the boys, not looks
That her girlfriends at school were thought of as losers.

So, the lesson is, sisters, she'll respect what you taught her
Despite contradictions have faith in your daughter
You'll just about live through that day in the summer
When you too may be labelled "Rose Queen's mother"

Penny Windsor

Things Men Say[2]

men in the street say funny things
here are some of their sayings
"get 'em off"
"hello big tits"
"fancy a bit darling"
"smile"
"get it up there"
"your place or mine"
this is a brief selection

now, I don't want to be difficult
unappreciative
I know these are all sayings
that mean I'm desirable
wanted by men
in a man's world
this is obviously a good thing
and it's not that I want intellectual conversation
or the New Man's heavy sensitivity
or even gems of common wisdom from the building site ...
but I do feel
and I don't want to offend anyone
the standard's a bit low
I'm sorry for all this
because I know men try
they really do
and it's very confusing to know what women want
but I think ... and I do apologise
that these sayings
don't ... amuse or excite me
or even make me feel ... attractive
and if I'm completely honest
and don't misunderstand me
I'm not a feminist
if I'm completely honest
these sayings irritate
in fact
they make me Angry
yes, ANGRY
I wish those men would stuff their little sayings
in their lunch box
sorry about that.

Penny Windsor

Some Observations About Women Travelling Alone[3]

women can eat at a cafe or restaurant
women can't picnic in a public square
can - drink coffee in a cafe but not beer in a bar

women can sit and read, or write a novel
but women can't just sit

women can walk quickly and purposefully in one particular
    direction
but they can't go past the same place twice within a short time
    for no apparent reason
or stand still for no apparent reason
women can stand still if they look at an historic building or in a
    shop window

women can go out after dark to visit relatives or do late night
    shopping
they cannot walk round generally after dark

they can travel with a particular and worthy and feminine
    reason in mind
such as collecting butterflies
but they cannot travel to wander or merely to sightsee

women can wear loose clothes in dark or pastel shades
but not tightfitting and revealing clothes in any colour
or loose clothes in bright colours

women can smile and look directly at children and dogs
women cannot smile or look directly at men

women by themselves can mention their husbands,
    boyfriends, children with fondness and regret
they cannot say they are alone by choice
oh no, they can never say they are alone by choice

Penny Windsor

Whatweakersex?[4]

There's one thing I've always wanted to do
cos I think it'd be such fun.
It's to go round pinching every man I see
firmly on the bum.
To watch them blush and edge away
would be my greatest thrill.
On tubes and crowded pavements
I'd be out to kill.
I'd pull a hefty handful of flesh
from off their manly cheek,
or perhaps I'd try a simpler style
and perfect a gentle tweak.
Denim bums and pin stripe bums
I'd give them all fair share,
a pinch just hard enough to prove
that tweaker sex was there

Fran Landsman

A Battered wife[5]

Purple, black ... all shades of love
Kicked into a patchwork on my body.
'Sorry' being a much longed for word:
But not to 'half a woman', 'a nobody',
No longer a wife, just a 'thing'.

A nothing, a walking ache.
Love could help, his love ...
But not friends, or doctors.
Outsiders being the final mistake.
Hanging together by the fear
Not the ultimate peace of death,
But the fear of being totally unloved,
Not being answered 'Why?' until
His fingers on my throat stop my breath.
Legs, body, back, head, breasts
Connected to me by strings of pain,
Just a puppet devoid of a soul
Dangling inside a black wedding frame.

Kate Thompson

Classroom Politics[6]

They will not forgive us
These girls
Sitting in serried rows
Hungry for attention
Like shelves of unread books,
If we do not
Make the world new for them,
Teach them to walk
Into the possibilities
Of their own becoming,
Confident in their exploring.
They will not forget
If we do not use
Our often-surrendered positions
On the front line
To wage war against
The subtle hordes of male historians
Who constantly edit female experience
And endlessly anthologise
Their own achievements.
They will not accept
The old excuses of their foremothers
If they grow up to find
That we have betrayed them

Fiona Norris

Nice Men[7]

I know a nice man who is kind to his wife and always lets her
do what she wants.

I heard of another nice man who killed his girlfriend. It was
an accident. He pushed her in a quarrel and she split open
her skull on the dining-room table. He was such a
guilt-ridden sight in court that the jury felt sorry for him.

My friend Aiden is nice. He thinks women are really equal.

There are lots of nice men who help their wives with the
shopping and the housework.

And many men, when you are alone with them, say,'I prefer
women. They are so understanding.' This is another
example of men being nice.

Some men, when you make a mistake at work, just laugh.
    They don't go on about it or shout. That's nice.

At times, the most surprising men will say at parties, 'There's
    a lot to this Women's Lib'. Here again, is a case of men
    behaving in a nice way.

Another nice thing is that some men are sympathetic when
    their wives feel unhappy.
I've often heard men say, 'Don't worry about everything so much, dear.'

You hear stories of men who are far more than nice - putting
    women in lifeboats first, etc.

Sometimes when a man has not been nice, he apologises and
    trusts you with intimate details of the pressures of his life.
    This just shows how nice he is, underneath.

I think that is all I can say on the subject of nice men. Thank
    you.

                                                            Dorothy Byrne

Nursery rhymes, folk songs and music

Some nursery rhymes provide discussion topics for both young children and older
students about how women and girls, men and boys are represented. Whilst we present
rhymes such as these uncritically, children will not be given the chance to challenge
the stereotyped roles they face. Apart from these ones listed below, many pop records
and videos use sexist language, gender-stereotyping and sexist images. Once the
students are aware of the nature and extent of sexism they may well be able to bring in
examples of current hits to discuss and share.

Recently I was invited to attend a school's production of *'The Boyfriend'* by Sandy
Wilson. This popular musical, depicting life in a girls' finishing school in the 1920s,
is often chosen by schools because of the music, the dancing and the energy which can
come out of such a production. Yet it would be one of the most sexist scores around.
But this is not to say that such musicals should not be contemplated. It is exactly this
type of work which can provide the stimulation for a programme on sexual equality,
sexual harassment or sexual discrimination. In turn this could lead to research being
done on, for example, the suffrage movement in Britain in 1920, as a contrast to the
attitudes and values inherent in the musical.

Little Polly Flinders

Little Polly Flinders
Sat among the cinders
Warming her pretty little toes
Her mother came and caught her
And whipped her naughty daughter
For spoiling her nice new clothes.

Curly Locks

Curly Locks, Curly Locks,wilt thou be
mine?
Thou shalt not wash dishes, nor yet feed
the swine,
But sit on a cushion and sew a fine seam,
And feed upon strawberries, sugar and
cream.

Georgie Porgie

Georgie Porgie Pudding and Pie
Kissed the girls and made them cry.
When the boys came out to play
Georgie Porgie ran away.

Little Miss Muffet

Little Miss Muffet, sat on a tuffet
Eating her curds and whey,
There came a big spider, that sat down
beside her,
And frightened Miss Muffet away.

The Farmer

The farmer's in the Dell,
The farmer's in the Dell,
Ee, ie, adio
The farmer's in the Dell.

The farmer wants a wife
The farmer wants a wife
Ee, ie, adio
The farmer wants a wife.

The wife wants a child.
The child wants a nurse.
The nurse wants a dog.
The dog wants a bone.
We all pat the bone.

O Soldier, Soldier

'O Soldier, soldier, won't you marry me?
With your musket fife and drum?'
'Oh no sweet maid I cannot marry thee,
For I have no coat/hat/glove/boots to put
on!'
Then up she went to her grandfather's
chest,
And got him a coat/hat/glove/boots of
the very, very best,
She got him a coat/hat/glove/boots of
the very, very best,
And the soldier put it on.

'O Soldier, soldier, won't you marry me?
With your musket fife and drum?'
'Oh no sweet maid I cannot marry thee,
For I have a wife of my own!'

Song: O No John!

1

On yonder hill there stands a creature
Who she is I do not know,
I'll go and court her for her beauty;
She must answer Yes or No.
O No John! No John! No John! No!

2

My father was a Spanish captain
Went to sea a month ago,
First he kissed me, then he left me
Bid me always answer No.
O No John! No John! No John! No!

3

O Madam in your face is beauty,
On your lips red roses grow,
Will you take me for your lover?
Madam answer Yes or No.
O No John! No John! No John! No!

4

O Madam I will give you jewels;
I will make you rich and free;
I will give you silken dresses,
Madam will you marry me?
O No John! No John! No John! No!

5

Oh Madam, since you are so cruel,
And that you do scorn me so,
If I may not be your lover,
Madam, will you let me go?
O No John! No John! No John! No!

6

Then I will stay with you forever,
If you will not be unkind,
Madam, I have vowed to love you;
Would you have me change my mind?
O No John! No John! No John! No!

7

O hark! I hear the church bells ringing:
Will you come and be my wife?
Or, dear Madam, have you settled
To be single all your life?
O No John! No John! No John! No!

Different methods of child care

Many people believe that it is the mother's responsibility, solely, to care for and bring up the children in a family, and that somehow she is born with the necessary temperament, characteristics and skills to do this. However, mothers staying at home is a relatively modern phenomenon. Throughout history children have usually been minded by people other than their mothers. In the upper-classes a variety of people were employed. Nannies looked after very young children. Governesses were engaged to supervise them when they were older or, in the case of boys, the children, even as young as 7, were sent away to boarding schools. In the working classes where women had to work all day other family members were charged with the babies' care.

Wet Nurses

In nineteenth-century Paris and other major French cities, working-class women customarily placed their babies for a year or more to board with rural wet nurses so they could continue to supplement the family income. By 1869 it was estimated that about 40 % of the 55,000 children born in Paris that year were being nursed or cared for by commercial wet nurses in the countryside.

In the London Daily Telegraph in 1866, advertisements could be found from both wealthy women wanting wet nurses and from young women wanting positions as wet nurses.

'Nurse - wet - nurse wanted, to take charge of an infant. Must be healthy and single. Apply for address at the Post-office, 65, Marsham-street, Westminster'. (*The Daily Telegraph,* September 14th, 1866).

'Wet Nurse - A respectable healthy young woman from the country with an excellent breast of milk (infant a few days old) desires a situation as above. Address MA Post office, Judd-street, W.C'. (*The Daily Telegraph,* 2nd November, 1866).

Slave Motherhood

'My Aunt Mary b'longed to Marse (Master) John Craddock and when his wife died and left a little baby - dat was little Miss Lucy - Aunt Mary was nussin' a new baby of her own, so Marse John made her let his baby suck too. If Aunt Mary was feedin' her own baby and Miss Lucy started cryin' Marse John would snatch her baby up by the legs and spank him, and tell Aunt Mary to go and nuss his baby fust. Aunt Mary couldn't answer him a word, but my ma said she offen seed Aunt Mary cry 'til de tears met under her chin'. Hellerstein *et al* (1981, p. 231).

Charles Dickens: David Copperfield

When his mother marries Mr Murdstone, David Copperfield comes into conflict with his new step-father and step-aunt. After a number of months the situation worsens and when David fails to satisfy Mr Murdstone's educational standards he is severely beaten. During the beating he bites his stepfather and, as a result is sent to boarding school.

Boarding School

'I should think there never can be a man who enjoyed his profession more than Mr. Creakle did. He had a delight in cutting at the boys, which was like the satisfaction of a craving appetite. I am confident that he couldn't resist a chubby boy, especially: that there was a fascination in such a subject, which made him restless in his mind, until he had scored and marked him for the day. I was chubby myself, and ought to know' C. Dickens (undated, p.116)

Penny Leach

In a book written in the late 1970s, especially for mothers with young babies, it is interesting to see how attitudes to child-rearing have changed. In this extract Leach talks about a child's first entry into the world outside the home. Note the use of the pronoun 'he'.

Launching into life
'His *(sic)* journeys are all outwards now, into that waiting world. But he feels the invisible and infinitely elastic threads that still guide him back to you. He returns to the base that is you, seeking rest and re-charging for each new leap into life'. P. Leach (1979, p. 444)

Different perspectives on wolf-whistling

In September 1990, an article appeared in the Cambridge Evening News. It said that the City Council had developed a policy on sexual harassment and that this behaviour would no longer be tolerated in its employees. Employees who used sexual harassment could be sacked. Further, according to the newspaper report, council workmen caught whistling at women in Cambridge could face disciplinary procedures. In the same article eight people were asked their opinion of wolf-whistles.

Wolf-whistles
'Mrs Turner, 28, said, "I usually try to ignore it. I find that attitude normally works better than answering back. I do find it embarrassing. We would not dream of doing it to a man, so why should they try to humiliate us?"

Mrs Bond, 45, said, "Building sites are the worst. It doesn't bother me that much because I usually wear trousers and flat shoes, so I can make a quick getaway. But if I was alone and dressed up I would be very embarrassed. To discipline someone for doing it would be ridiculous".

Miss Roberts, 18, said, "It is annoying. I go to a school in London, and if you go past in your school uniform you are greeted by all sorts of taunts. I stick two fingers up or ignore it, but it would be over the top to sack someone".

Miss Garrity, 25, said, "If you are a young single woman I think it is more flattering. But if you are attached it's just a nuisance, you just feel like you are being harassed. My mum would give them a mouthful back".

Miss Dean, 18, said, "I actually think it's flattering. It proves that they think you are attractive -- it's like when cars toot you. And if they are good looking, it's even better. I certainly don't think anyone should get the sack over it".

Mr Lankaster, 37, said, "If I see an attractive girl with a good figure I'll whistle. It embarrasses some of them, but it's just a tease. Some of them give us a verbal response, others turn away, some laugh. One woman gave us a twirl".

Mr Nunn, 20, said, "It would be a bit extreme to sack someone for doing it. If I've got a spare moment and I see someone good-looking I'll whistle. It's just our way of being friendly, and I think some of them appreciate it. I just wish the girls would do it to us"' (*Cambridge Evening News*, September 7, 1990).

Resources for students

Here is a list of books for children. In some there are characters which challenge the stereotypes of aggressive, adventurous boys and passive cocoa-making girls providing a wider spectrum of behaviour models. Others are clearly fun books which turn gender-stereotyping on its head and present whacky and unique characters of both sexes. However, whilst some books on the market these days are purportedly 'non-sexist', many are confusing and have contradictory messages for students.

Some of the best discussions I have had are those which arise out of sexist books. As most schools do not have the resources to buy new books, fairy tales, nursery rhymes and Enid Blyton's stories can give much scope for discussions about gender stereotyping.

For current and newly published non-sexist books for children, there is a company called the Letterbox Library which specialises in this area. Their address is Unit 2 D, Leroy House, 436, Essex Road, London, N1 3QP.

For non-sexist materials for boys contact Whyld Publishing Co-op, Moorland House, Caistor, Lincs LNF 6SF. They specialise in packs, posters, games as well as curriculum materials.

Ahlberg, A. (1980) *Mrs Plug the Plumber*. Harmondsworth: Puffin (4-8 years).

Ahlberg, J. and Ahlberg, A. (1977) *Burglar Bill*. London: Heinemann (3-7 years).

Chick, S. (1987) *Push Me, Pull Me*. London: The Women's Press (14-18 years).

Cole, B. (1986) *Princess Smartypants*. London: Collins (5-9 years).

Kaye, G. (1984) *Comfort Herself*. London: Andre Deutsch (9-13 years).

Kemp, G. (1977 rpt 1979) *The Turbulent Term of Tyke Tiler*. Harmondsworth: Puffin (9-14 years).

Little, J. (1984) *Mama's Going to Buy You a Mockingbird*. Harmondsworth: Puffin (11-15 years).

Lurie, A. (1980) *Clever Gretchen and Other Folk Tales*. London: Heinemann (all levels).

Mark, J. (1983) *Handles*. Harmondsworth: Puffin (12-15 years).

Mark, J. (1985) *Trouble Half-way*. Harmondsworth: Puffin (11-15 years).

Munsch, R. (1982) *The Paperbag Princess*. London: Hippo Press (4-10 years).

Ormerod, J. (1984) *101 Things to do with a Baby*. Harmondsworth: Kestrel (all levels).

Paterson, K. (1977) *Bridge to Terabithia*. Harmondsworth: Puffin (9-13 years).

Paterson, K. (1980) *Jacob have I loved*. Harmondsworth: Puffin (9-13 years).

Paterson, K. (1988) *Park's Quest*. Harmondsworth: Puffin (11-14 years).

Pearce, P. (1983) *The Way to Sattin Shore*. Harmondsworth: Puffin. (9-13 years).

Phelps, E.J. (1981) *The Maid of the North; feminist folk tales from around the world*. New York: Holt. (12-18 years).

Ross, T. (1978) *Little Red Riding Hood*. Harmondsworth: Puffin (4-10 years).

Steel, S. and Styles, M. (1990) (eds.) *Mother Gave a Shout; poems by women and girls*. London: A and C Black (all levels).

Smith, L. (1990) *Equality: Understanding Feminism*. London: Collins (14-18 years).

Voigt, C. (1981) *Homecoming*. London: Collins (10-14 years).

Voigt, C. (1982 rpt 1990) *Dicey's Song*. London: Harper Collins (10-14 years).

Wharton, M. (1990) *Understanding Social Issues: Abortion*. London: Gloucester Press (13-18 years).

Zolotow, C. (1972) *William's Doll*. New York: Harper/Row (3-7 years).

References

[1] Dangerous Women (1987) Penny Windsor, honno poetry, Ailsa Craig, Hoel y Cawl, Dinas Powys, South Glamorgan, CF6 4AH

[2] Ibid.

[3] Ibid.

[4] Taken from *No Holds Barred: The Raving Beauties Choose New Poems by Women,* London: The Women's Press,1985.

[5] Ibid.

[6] Ibid.

[7] Ibid.

Bibliography

In this bibliography there are references I have used and from which I have quoted, as well as other books which are useful as background reading in gender issues in the classroom.

Archer, J. and Lloyd, B. (1982) *Sex and Gender.* Harmondsworth: Penguin.

Askew, S. and Ross, C. (1988) *Boys Don't Cry: Boys and Sexism in Education.* Milton Keynes: Open University Press.

de Beauvoir, S. (1949 rpt 1984) (Trans. and ed. H.M. Parshley) *The Second Sex.* Harmondsworth: Penguin.

Brontë, C. (1966) *Jane Eyre,* introduction and notes by Q.D. Leavis. Harmondsworth: Penguin.

Commission for Racial Equality (1987) *Training: The implementation of equal opportunities at work* (Vol 2. Case Studies). Elliot House, 10/12 Allington Sreet, London SW1E 5EH.

Dickens, C. (undated) *David Copperfield.* London: Chapman and Hall and Humphrey Milford.

Dziech, B.W. and Weiner, L. (1984) *The Lecherous Professor; Sexual Harassment on Campus.* Boston: Beacon Press.

Farley, L. (1978 rpt 1980) *Sexual Shakedown. The Sexual Harassment of Women on the Job.* New York: Warner Books.

Geis, R. Wright, R. and Geis, G. (1984) 'Police Officer or Doctor? Police Surgeons' Attitudes and Opinions about Rape'. In J.Hopkins (ed.), op. cit.

Grabrucker, M. (1988) *There's a Good Girl: Gender stereotyping in the first three years of life: A Diary.* London: The Women's Press.

Hadjifotou, N. (1983) *Women and Harassment at Work.* London: Pluto Press.

Hanmer, J. and Maynard, M. (1987) (eds.) *Women, Violence and Social Control.* Basingstoke: Macmillan.

Hanmer, J. and Saunders, S. (1984) *Well Founded Fear. A Community Study of Violence to Women*. London: Hutchinson in association with The Explorations in Feminism Collective.

Hardy, T. (1891, rpt 1984). *Tess of the d'Urbervilles*. London: Dent and Sons.

Hellerstein, E.O., Hume, L.P. and Offen, K.M. (1981) (eds.) *Victorian Women. A Documentary Account of Women's Lives in Nineteenth-Century England, France, and the United States*. Stanford, California: Stanford University Press.

Herbert, C.M.H. (1989) *Talking of Silence: the Sexual Harassment of Schoolgirls*. Basingstoke: Falmer Press.

Hopkins, J. (1984)(ed.) *Perspectives on Rape and Sexual Assault*. London: Harper/Row.

Ingliss, A.A.H. (1971) *A Selection from Phoenix*. Harmondsworth: Peregrine.

Jacobs, H.A. (1987) *Incidents in the Life of a Slave Girl*. Cambridge, MA: Harvard University Press.

Kramarae, C. and Treichler, P.A. (1985) *Feminist Dictionary*. London: Pandora Press.

Lawrence, D.H. (1966) *Women in Love*. Harmondsworth: Penguin.

Lowe, M. (1984) 'The Role of the Judiciary in the Failure of the Sexual Offences (Amendment) Act to Improve the Treatment of the Rape Victim', in J.Hopkins (ed.) op. cit.

Leach, P. (1979) *Baby and Child*. Harmondsworth: Penguin.

MacKinnon, C.A. (1979) *Sexual Harassment of Working Women*. New Haven: Yale University Press.

Mahony, P. (1984) *Schools for the Boys: Coeducation Reassessed*. London: Hutchinson in association with The Explorations in Feminism Collective.

Mead, M. (1949 rpt 1981) *Male and Female*. Harmondsworth: Penguin.

Millett, K. (1970 rpt 1983) *Sexual Politics*. London: Virago Press.

NASUWT (1990) *Sexual Harassment: Action for Equality*.

National Association for the Teaching of English, Language and Gender Working Party. (1985) *Alice in Genderland: Reflections on Language, Power and Control*. NATE, 49, Broomgrove Road, Sheffield, S10 2NA.

National Curriculum Council (1990) *Curriculum Guidance 3: The Whole Curriculum,* York: NCC.

National Union of Teachers: *Dealing with Sexual Harassment: Guidelines for Teachers.*

Newsom, J. (1963) *Half Our Future: A Report of the Central Advisory Council for Education (England).* London: Her Majesty's Stationery Office.

Nicholson, J. (1984) *Men and Women. How different are they?* Oxford: Oxford University Press.

Rapoport, R., Rapoport, R. and Strelitz, Z. (1977) *Fathers, Mothers and Others.* London: Routledge and Kegan Paul.

Raving Beauties (1985) (eds.) *No Holds Barred; The Raving Beauties Choose New Poems by Women.* London: The Women's Press

Read, J. (1988) *The Equal Opportunities Book.* London: Interchange Books.

Read, S. (1982) *Sexual Harassment at Work.* London: Hamlyn.

Rousseau, J-J. (1762 rpt 1984) *Emile.* London: John Dent.

Seager, J. and Olson, A. (1986) *Women in the World; An International Atlas.* London: Pan Books.

Sheffield Men Against Sexual Harassment (1984) S.M.A.S.H. *An Information Pack for Men: Sexual Harassment, Rape and Sexual Abuse of Children.* Available from MAGIC (Men Against Gender Injustice Collective), P.O. Box 142, Sheffield S1 3HG.

South Australian Department of Education (1984) *Sexual Harassment.* S.A. Ed. Dept, Flinders Street, Adelaide S.A. 5000.

Spender, D. and Sarah, E. (1980) (eds.) *Learning To Lose.* London: The Women's Press.

Spender, D. (1980) *Man Made Language.* London: Routledge and Kegan Paul.

Spender, D. (1981) (ed.) *Men's Studies Modified: The Impact of Feminism on the Academic Disciplines.* Oxford: Pergamon.

Spender, D. (1982) *Invisible Women: The Schooling Scandal.* London: Writers and Readers Cooperative Society.

Stones, R. (1983) *Pour Out the Cocoa, Janet: Sexism in Children's Books.* Harlow: Longman.

Swann Report (1985) *Education for All, Committee of Enquiry into the Education of Children from Ethnic Minority Groups*, Cmnd 9453, London HMSO.

Szirom, T. and Dyson, S. (1986) *Greater Expectations: A source book for working with girls and young women.* Wisbech: Learning Development Aids.

Trades Union Congress (1983) *Sexual Harassment of Women at Work: A Study from West Yorkshire/Leeds Trade Union and Community Research and Information Centre.* Trades Union Congress, Congress House, Great Russell Street, London WC1B 3LS.

Tutchell, E. (1990) (ed.) *Dolls and Dungarees: Gender Issues in the Primary School Curriculum.* Milton Keynes: Open University Press.

Walker, B.G. (1983) *The Woman's Encyclopedia of Myths and Secrets.* New York: Harper/Row.

Walkerdine, V. (1990) *Schoolgirl Fictions.* London: Verso

Weiner, G. (1985) (ed.) *Just a Bunch of Girls.* Milton Keynes: Open University Press.

Whitbread, A. (1980) 'Female Teachers are Women First: Sexual Harassment at Work'. in D. Spender and E. Sarah, *Learning to Lose.* op cit.

Whyld, J. (1983) (ed.) *Sexism in the Secondary Curriculum.* London: Harper/Row.

Windsor, P. (1987) *Dangerous Women.* honno poetry, Ailsa Craig, Hoel y Cawl, Dinas Powys, South Glamorgan, CF6 4AH.

Wise, S. and Stanley, L. (1987) *Georgie Porgie: Sexual Harassment in Everyday Life.* London: Pandora Press.

Index

The Daily Telegraph, 99
The Guardian, 21
The Taming of the Shrew, 89
The Times, 5, 6
Theatre in Education, 48
'Tomboys', 17
Touching, 30, 75
Toys, 17, 31
Trivialisation, 51, 69
Typical boys, 33

United Nations Report, 46
Universities, 24, 35, 37, 64, 86
Upper-classes, 34, 98

Victim, see sexual harassment, recipients of
Victimisation, 49, 83

Vignettes, vi, 79-81

Wage earners, 7, 11
Walkerdine, Valerie, 39
Weiner, L., 24
West, Rebecca, 44
Whyld, Janie, 32
Wilson, Sandy, 96
Wise, Sue, 25
Wives, 28
Wolf-whistle, 21, 40, 43, 44, 71, 74, 76, 100
Women,
-- as sexual objects, 22, 84
-- as workers, 7, 8, 19
Woodwork, 85
Working-classes, 34, 98
Workplace, 12, 20